Wingshooting
More Birds in Your Bag

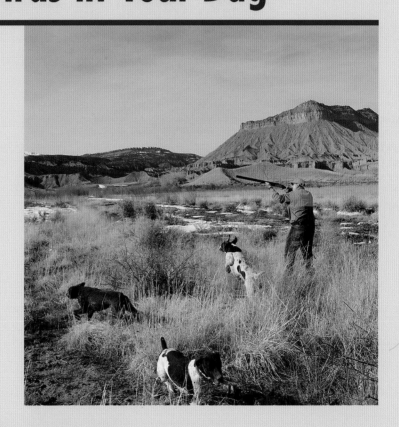

PETER F. BLAKELEY

STACKPOLE
BOOKS

Published by
STACKPOLE BOOKS
5067 Ritter Road
Mechanicsburg, PA 17055
www.stackpolebooks.com

Printed in China

First edition

Photos by the author except where noted.

10 9 8 7 6 5 4 3 2 1

Library of Congress Cataloging-in-Publication Data

Blakeley, Peter F.
    Wingshooting / Peter F. Blakeley. — 1st ed.
        p.   cm.
    Includes index.
    ISBN 978-0-8117-0566-0 (hardcover) — ISBN 0-8117-0566-8 (hardcover)
1. Fowling. I. Title.
SK313.B54   2012
799.2'4—dc23
                                                           2012002414

To Alison, the best wife
in the world, with love

Contents

Preface

Shotgunning books are magnets for bird hunters. There's a good chance that if you've picked this one up, you're already a dedicated sportsman and love to hunt. Perhaps you would like to learn more about shotgunning skills so you can put more birds in your bag. If that's the case, please read on. But if you expect this to be a book full of lots of pictures of me and others sitting on piles of birds and brandishing expensive shotguns, I'm afraid you will be disappointed.

At the time of this writing, dozens of such books are out there, all promising to transform you instantly into a better bird hunter. But there are very few, to my knowledge, that have been written by a full-time, professional shooting coach. That doesn't mean that I know everything there is to know about hunting quail, doves, pheasants, ducks and geese, and the like, but over the years, I have hunted my fair share of them all. More important, I have coached a massive number of clients, from all walks of life, who enjoy bird hunting. If the feedback from them is anything to go by, they have all gleaned a scrap of something useful from my coaching, some modicum of enlightenment that they personally extracted from my professional knowledge, that helped them to put an extra bird or two in their bags.

All the stories and techniques in this book come from my real experiences in the field and from coaching seminars with clients on both sides of the Atlantic. Some of the hunting stories are from Scotland and some are from here in the US. The art and science of shotgunning knows no boundaries. It makes no difference if a handsome rooster pheasant erupts from the barley stubble in the Scottish lowlands or the golden shimmering sea of the Kansas cornfield. The knowledge and technique you need to apply to harvest him is the same in each case.

So how, exactly, did I accumulate all this knowledge? When I was a kid, firearms and fishing rods were a distraction for me. Firearms especially were fascinatingly seductive. Both my parents were apprehensive about guns and, at first, would not allow me to own one. Just about the only thing I had on my side was spirit and enthusiasm. But primeval stirrings were within me, and the thrill of the chase was in my blood. I had aspirations to be a shooter, to be a bird hunter. The thrill of the hunt embraced me; I had absolutely no choice in the matter. Other kids yearned to be doctors or lawyers. I was different. Everything I did in those days involved fishing rods or guns, and my waking hours were filled with the illogical joy that only a hunter can experience as his hand-eye choreography succeeds and he brings down a flying bird with his shotgun.

My first gun was a Diana .177 air rifle, followed by a Webley and Scott bolt action .410. Both guns were secreted away from my parents, wrapped in one of my father's old tweed jackets and stored under the pile of coal in the air-raid shelter at the bottom of the garden.

I acquired my first 12 gauge when I was eleven. My uncle had a farm in Stoke-on-Trent in the north of England, and one day during the summer when I was visiting the farm my younger cousin William showed me the gun. It was hidden away in a dark recess in the roof of one of the barns that we called the "cat loft." I drooled over the gun. It was an ancient, rusted, Damascus-barreled Thomas Horsley that had seen better days.

The gun, in fact, was a death trap, a gunsmith's nightmare. The action was so loose that it rattled, and the top lever had to be held across to stop it from opening. I later "fixed" the problem by stretching a loop of elastic (stolen from a pair of my big sister's knickers!) between the top lever and the trigger guard. Cousin William was forbidden to touch the gun and swore me to secrecy, but I took it apart and sneaked it into my father's Norton motorbike and sidecar for the return trip to Manchester.

I was fearful all the way home that I would be found out and the gun would be confiscated, but it wasn't. When the coast was clear, I transferred the gun to a more secure place. Once again, the air-raid shelter at the bottom of our garden served as a hidey-hole. This time, I slipped the gun inside a roll of old, moldy, moth-eaten carpet that had been lying along the top of a set of ladders for as long as I could remember. In those days, most families were eking out a frugal existence and almost nothing was discarded just in case it would come in useful someday. When my dad was at work, I lovingly cleaned and overlubricated the ancient action with his oil can and lovingly caressed the gun, swinging it at imaginary rabbits and birds as often as possible. Sundays were always gardening day.

"Our Peter!" Dad would bellow frustratingly, "Have you seen my oil can? I need it to oil the lawn mower!"

"No, Dad," I would lie, wearing my best picture of innocence. "I haven't seen it." I didn't have the heart (or courage!) to tell him.

In those days I lived in Stockport, Cheshire, England, within a stone's throw of Lord Egerton's estate, Tatton Hall. Throughout the summer

months, the keepers on the estate relied heavily on local boy power, and during the summer school breaks, accompanied by like-minded others, my friends and I pedaled our bikes along the leafy Cheshire lanes to the estate to help the keepers.

We were never bored; there was always a pheasant pen to mend, ditch to clean, nesting box to repair, moles to trap, or rabbits to snare. The hen coops, where the broody hens hatched the pheasant eggs, needed to be scrubbed clean and sterilized each season. That was hard work for us, and we received no payment for our toils. Instead, we were allowed to make good use of the estate fields and lakes.

We fished for pike and perch and hunted or trapped vermin to the exclusion of everything else. We were wild, unkempt, grubby individuals and anything that could be caught with a fishing rod or shot with an air rifle became our quarry. We were allowed to keep rabbits and pigeons and soon made a lucrative business out of it—we could get three pence each for a rabbit or pigeon and six pence for a hare.

Pike were considered a nuisance because they took the young ducklings. We caught them with set lines baited with small roach. Pike and perch were good eating, and we could get six pence a pound for them.

But the real reward for all of us was the invitation to the keeper's day at the end of the season. On keeper's day we were allowed to shoot the quarry that the gentry had paid a pretty penny for . . . the pheasants and partridges.

It was only on the keeper's shoots that we were allowed to use a shotgun, for safety's sake, under the watchful eye of our keepers. On the allotted day, we would all be taut as bowstrings, excited and apprehensive as we lined up along the ancient rides of mighty oaks and beech trees. No longer resplendent in their autumn foliage, the now starkly skeletal trees had shed most of their leaves, covering the woodland with a rich blanket of russet, gold, and brown. Dressed in these same colors, myriad pheasants, cockling with complaints as they came, skimmed off over the tops of the trees.

I was making heavy going of it, and most of the birds were sailing by unscathed. My mentor at that time was Andy Mcloud, a Scottish expat with a shock of amber hair and a face as red and shiny as a ripe tomato. At the keeper's shoot, I had borrowed one of Andy's guns for the day. Andy stood in silence, watching my pitiful attempt to connect as the birds came over me. Eventually, he offered some advice.

"Can you see the birds, laddie?" he posed the question.

"Aye, Andy," I nodded meekly, "I can see the birds."

Andy raised his eyebrows slightly and then added, "So you can see where they're going then?"

"Aye, Andy," I nodded, "I can see where they're going."

"Well then, shoot where they're going, not where they've been, laddie!"

Of course, I didn't believe Andy. I was young, impetuous, and inexperienced. I was making two of the mistakes that almost everyone makes when they use a shotgun—looking at the bead on the end of the gun and shooting directly at the birds. As my frustration increased and more of the birds "cocked a snoot" as they sailed on by, in desperation, I reluctantly decided I would do as Andy suggested.

The next bird to come over me was right on time. It was a splendid cock pheasant that rattled his way out of his tangled cover of blackberry and bracken, his powerful pinions propelling him like a russet rocket across the tops of the trees. Overflowing with trepidation as I watched his approach, I hesitantly brought my gun up to intercept him. This time, under Andy's scrutinizing gaze, just as I triggered the shot, I pointed my gun at a spot slightly in front of my quarry and pulled the trigger. The magnificent bird folded like a bad poker hand . . . and nobody was more surprised than me.

I turned and looked at Andy. He rarely smiled, but now he was grinning like a loon and simply shrugged his broad shoulders. It was a valuable lesson that I remember still. The remainder of the day went well, and before too long, the birds began fluttering from the sky like spent confetti at your sister's wedding.

In later years, I had the privilege and pleasure to shoot on some of the best estates in Scotland, including the Duke of Buccleuch's estate in Langholm, where I had a gun shop, Border Tackle and Guns. I was the shooting coach at Annandale Shooting Ground in Dumfriesshire and later, on this side of the Atlantic, Westside Sporting Grounds in Houston and the Dallas Gun Club, arguably one of the finest shooting facilities in the world.

To become a successful shotgunner, you must, over a period of time, build up a personal mental repertoire of sight pictures, a library of images you know to be correct. We call these sight pictures bird/barrel relationships. To do this, we need to consider three variables. The first variable is the flight line, or trajectory, of the bird. Finding the line of the bird should be easy to do; it is the two-dimensional segment that we perceive the bird to be travelling along relative to our eyes. The second variable is the speed of the bird. The third variable is the range or distance to the bird. You need to consider these three variables to apply the correct amount of the ever-confusing, but necessary, illusive element—forward allowance or lead.

The initial stumbling block for many of us is how we decipher these variables. Wingshooting is irrefutably a hand-eye coordination sport. The best bird hunters learn, over time, to read the visual information and make it all look easy. Their hands and eyes work as a coordinated team, and they seem to have the uncanny knack of inserting their shotgun muzzles in exactly the right place to intercept their birds with consummate ease. Because birds are predictably unpredictable, many of us struggle with this, but with good instruction, we can all learn to do it.

Forward allowance, or lead, is always the primary stumbling block. On the Texas dove hunt, you notice a rapidly approaching gray speedster, throttling his way across the field of nodding sunflowers on the wings of the wind. You quickly lift the shotgun to your shoulder in an attempt to intercept him, but then you shake your head in bewilderment as your futile shot spurs him on into the next county. You rewind the shot and kick the variables around in your head. How much lead did he need?

You flush the wily woodcock, and as he extricates himself from the tangle of briars and cat's claw and ghosts away into the tangled thicket like a big brown moth, you throw the gun up and try to come to terms with him, but he never falters. What about him? How much lead did he need? Shooting coaches in the UK have a saying: "What's hit is history, what's missed is mystery." Very true.

In my younger days, I was primarily a hunter, not a shooting coach or a writer. I got sucked into coaching and writing because I love it, and of course, I still hunt, when I get the chance. But I also love to coach and teaching others in the art of shotgunning has been my full-time occupation now on both sides of the Atlantic for over 35 years. This book is a distillation of tips, techniques, and carefully compiled knowledge of the unit lead system that I have developed during this period, based on practical experience. I think you will find it useful.

My long-suffering wife, Alison, took most of the technical pictures for this book at the Elmfork Shooting Facility in Dallas. The owners of the facility, All-American Sporting Clays Champion Scott Robertson, co-owner Marc Richman, and manager Jeannie Almond, allow me to coach my clients there, and my gratitude to them is long, high, and wide.

Many people helped me with this book, and I hope I have not left anyone out. Many of the superb wingshooting pictures herein were taken by others. These include the excellent driven pheasant pictures that were provided by Jen and Lars Magnusson, taken at the premier driven pheasant shooting facility of Blixt & Co.

Jackson Hole, Wyoming, dove, duck, and quail pictures were provided by renowned outdoors writer Nick Sisely, and outfitter J. J. Kent from Kent Outdoors also provided duck hunting pictures. The flushing pheasant picture at the start of each chapter and other excellent pictures throughout the book were provided by premier hunting facility Castle Valley Outdoors in Utah. My thanks also to stocker Paul Hodgins, Boone Pickens, Arthur Patton, Walter Kilgo, Diggory Hadoke, Thomas Kier, and Barrett Reese.

Pete Blakeley
Dallas, Texas

CHAPTER 1

Safety in the Field

If a sportsman true you'd be, listen carefully to me,

Never, never let your gun, pointed be at anyone,

That it may unloaded be, matters not the least to me.

—*Commander Mark Beaufoy*

Before you decide to skip this chapter and move on to the "more important" issues, please let me explain. This is my fourth how-to shotgunning book, and the chapter on safety deservedly comes first in all my books. To be a successful bird hunter requires that you become familiar with and understand many things. You must know and recognize your quarry. You must know and control your dogs. But most of all, you must know and respect your shotguns. Over the years, you must form a close and personal bond with them. Guns mean serious business. Gun safety takes priority over everything, and before you learn to hunt and handle guns on a regular basis, you must learn to be intimately familiar with your guns. If you are not, you are a danger not only to yourself, but to your shooting companions and their dogs.

I have handled shotguns and firearms for over 50 years on both sides of the Atlantic, and I have been a full-time shooting coach for over 35 years. A good proportion of these 35 years was spent behind the counter of my gun and fishing tackle shop in the Scottish Borders. I was once handed a loaded gun across the shop counter by a gamekeeper who should have known better. This particular guy made light of the incident at the time, but I made it abundantly clear to him that it was not acceptable and he left the shop with severely assaulted ears. He never came back into the shop, and I was pleased and relieved that he didn't.

During that time, I never handed a gun to a customer unless it was proved to be open and empty. However, on two separate occasions, despite handling guns on an almost daily basis, I made mistakes. On both these occasions, nobody was injured, but the memory is burned indelibly into my mind and still haunts me today.

One thing that I have noticed over the years is that especially out in the field, shooters are much more at ease if they know that their shooting companions are safety conscious. Don't forget that we sometimes hunt in remote areas with no immediate access to medical facilities. Because of this, a bad accident can quickly escalate into a fatal one. Sometimes I have overheard others talking about a particular shooter who displays less than appropriate safety procedures as he handles his shotgun in hushed whispers, too embarrassed to say anything. They should not be. The shotgun is a devastatingly efficient weapon, designed for killing, and all guns can kill. All guns must be treated with caution and suspicion, and around guns, you must be constantly vigilant. These are fundamental facts; ones that must be observed and understood at all times. Some gun owners seem to almost resent being shown safety procedures, something that I have never fully understood. If you observe others handling guns in an unsafe manner, don't be too embarrassed to open your mouth and say something.

Become Familiar with Your Gun

The only way to become comfortable with handling a shotgun is to do just that. Handle it often . . . and I don't just mean for two days before the start of hunting season. You must mount it, carry it, open it, and familiarize yourself with the safety catch and feel of the trigger pull.

Empty it before you put it in and out of the gun slip and into the back of your vehicle. This should become a well-ingrained ritual. The correct way to take a gun from a gun slip is to slide your hand in to push the top lever across *before* removing it. Empty it and break it open before crossing a ditch, negotiating a fence, bending down to tie your shoelace, or removing a burr from the dog's paw.

Take it out to the shooting club and show it to your friends. Clean it regularly and become almost as familiar with it as you would a new girlfriend.

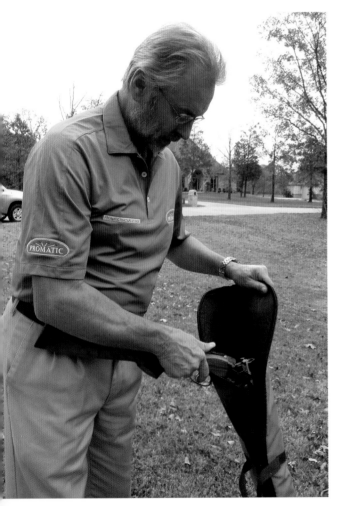

Open the top lever *before* you remove the gun from the slip. By doing this, others can see that the gun is empty and safe.

Not a good idea! This hunter decides to climb a gate with a loaded gun, and his finger is dangerously near the trigger. A sudden slip and the gun could be discharged with disastrous consequences. Open the gun and remove the shells before negotiating a fence or ditch.

You can apply manual safety catches, but that too can fail. The safety catch is a mechanical device and all mechanical devices can fail without warning, either through wear or negligence of the user.

The general principal of a safety catch is that the sear holds back the spring-loaded hammer. In normal use, pulling the trigger will not fire the gun when the safety is on, but the contact between the hammer and the sear is only slight. In an old gun, the sear can become worn over the years and any sharp impact, dropping the gun for example, can easily fire it. Because of this, shooting etiquette in the field should require guns to be carried open and empty at all times except when they are intended to be used.

Well, not exactly, but you get the picture. Only after you have handled the gun for some time will you develop muzzle awareness. Never allow the muzzles to stray in an errant direction.

There is no such thing as an automatic safety catch. Some guns are designed so that they should engage the safety every time they are opened, but don't depend completely on that. By the same rule, there is no such thing as a foolproof safety catch. That small S above the safety catch is a trap for the unwary. Don't rely on it.

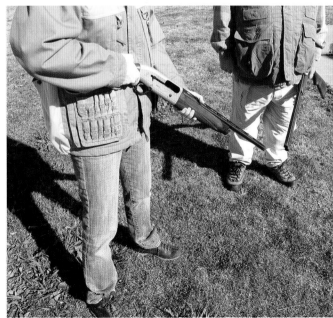

This gun is unloaded, but the muzzles are pointing at the feet of the other shooter and from where he is standing, he can't see that it's unloaded. Never allow the muzzles of a gun to stray in an errant direction.

In the Field

In the field, keep the safety on until you are ready to shoot. This should become part of your gun-mounting practice. Don't get in the habit of nervously clicking the safety catch on and off. With the side–by–side and over-and-under, remember "forward for fire," meaning that as you push the safety forward, the gun is made ready and you can do this by feel without looking at the safety. Most over-and-unders have the barrel selection on the safety catch, which can make it confusing initially until you familiarize yourself with the operation. With practice, this will become spontaneous and you can concentrate on the quarry instead of looking down at the gun. The seasoned bird hunter will select the barrel and push the safety off without conscious thought.

As you walk, occasionally check that the safety is engaged. Don't rely on the safety when negotiating fences or gates or hopping over ditches. Open the gun, unload it, and either pass it to

someone or place it in a safe position on the other side of the fence, gate, or ditch.

When lining out across a field during a push and block hunt, remain in line at all times. Glance occasionally to the left and right so you can speed up or slow down to synchronize your walking speed with that of your companions. Always know exactly where your companions are. This is particularly important when you are duck or goose hunting. Low shots as the birds come in across an expanse of water mean that a ricochet is a distinct possibility. Large shot sizes that are used for waterfowl can travel a long way, perhaps up to 500 yards. At this range, they may not be lethal, but a large pellet can still inflict enough damage to blind someone.

New shooters and youngsters should only be allowed one shell in hunting situations, until they have proved that they are trustworthy and capable of handling the gun. Novices and kids, especially when they hit what they are supposed to with the first shot, forget that they may have more than one shell in the gun and that it is ready to fire again. The early success at the first dove or quail can be short-lived, and excitement and overenthusiasm can sometimes result in a split second of carelessness that may have disastrous consequences. Don't forget also that extra vigilance is necessary when in wing hunting situations, because most wing hunting is carried out in remote areas with no immediate access to medical or hospital facilities. A bad accident can quickly turn into a fatal one in these situations. Load only when there is a possibility of seeing the quarry.

The safety catch is a mechanical device, and it can fail due to wear. Never rely on the safety catch when you place the gun in the back of a vehicle to move to an area that may be more productive. Always remove the shells first. If you can see the S on either an over-and-under or side-by-side, it means that the gun is safe. On a semiautomatic, the safety will probably be painted red. Always remember, S for safe and red for dead.

Stay in line with your companions.

Always unload when negotiating ditches and fences, stopping to tie a shoelace, or returning to the vehicle to move to a different spot. Applying the safety catch by itself is not acceptable.

Don't shoot when you can't identify your quarry clearly. Although I have seen people attempt to shoot quail through bushes, in my opinion this is dangerous and should be avoided. It's too late when a hurried shot at a quail in thick cover results in the loss of an eye or a faithful companion or shooting partner. All for the sake of one more bird in the bag? It isn't worth the risk. Always know the position of the other shooters, and when using dogs be even more vigilant. In the UK we have an area when walking up game that we call the safety zone. Any birds directly in front and approximately 45 degrees to the left and right of a walking gun are acceptable. This gives a 90-degree arc of fire and any birds in this area are considered to be fair game.

The proper procedure for loading a break-barrel gun (over-and-under, side-by-side) is to look down the barrels to check for obstructions before you use it. This is particularly important if the gun has been in storage for several months. I once had a client who almost loaded his favorite side-by-side at the start of a lesson but luckily discovered an obstruction just in time. This proved to be an unfortunate mouse, which had crawled up there during the close season, became lodged, and subsequently died! Firing the gun would have had disastrous results.

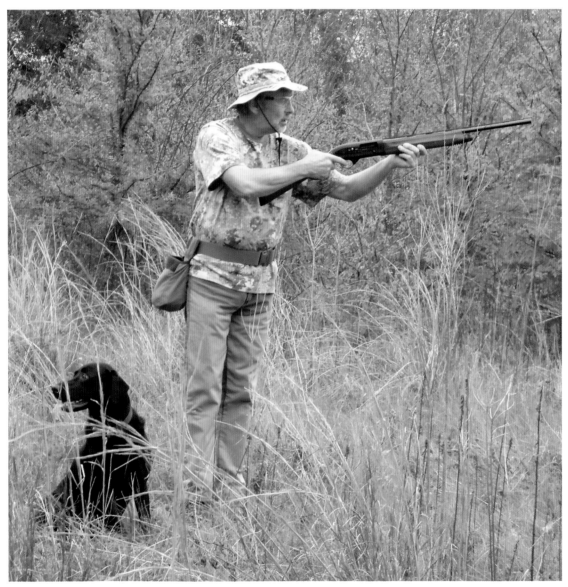

Don't shoot where you can't see! A low shot into the bushes in front is dangerous because a dog may be behind the cover, or worse, another hunter. Don't take the risk.

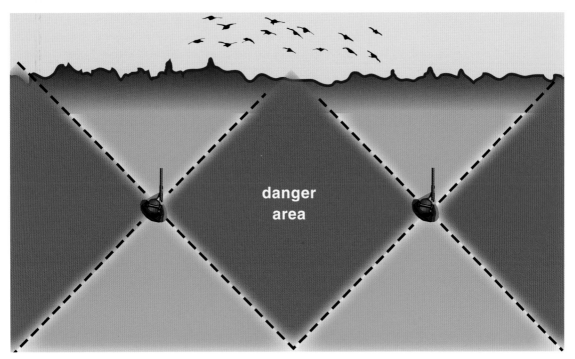

The arc of fire for both walked up and driven game is a 90-degree arc 45 degrees to the left and right of a walking gun. The shooter should never allow his gun to stray into the danger area.

Any shell that makes an abnormal sound as it goes off must be investigated to make sure the wad isn't lodged in the barrel. It is a good idea, in the field, to periodically check the barrels for obstruction. It isn't unusual for a duck or dove hunter to climb a fence and in the heat of the moment unwittingly stick his muzzles in the ground, blocking them with mud or snow.

Close the gun smoothly after you place the shells in the chamber; don't snap it shut with excessive force. A sticking firing pin is capable of firing the gun. Keep your trigger finger off the trigger, preferably along the trigger guard. Point the muzzles at the ground as you close the gun.

One of the things that I always ask my clients is if they know why 20-gauge shells are always yellow. The reason is of course so you can recognize them, but did you know that a 20-gauge shell fits neatly into the chamber of a 12 gauge and drops out of sight, making it possible to load a 12-gauge

shell on top and close the action? This makes a very efficient pipe bomb, because not only will the 12-gauge shell be detonated by the strike of the firing pin, but the 20-gauge shell will also be fired by the shot charge from the 12 gauge, producing a double detonation. The gun will almost certainly blow up in the unfortunate shooter's face! Husband and wife shooting partners take note! Don't ever mix his 12-gauge shells with her 20-gauge ones; the consequences will be disastrous.

Alcohol and guns don't mix. Even one beer is one too many. Hunting is a social occasion for many, and some think a few beers during the hunt is acceptable. I don't agree, but unfortunately, I have been on hunts where this is the normal routine. Don't foolishly believe that a beer or two at lunchtime will not impair your judgment because I assure you it will. Have as many as you like after the hunt, but not before. It just isn't worth the risk.

Don't mix ammo! If he is using a 12 gauge, a bird hunter wearing a shell pouch like this is asking for trouble! A 20-gauge shell will fit into a 12-gauge chamber and drop out of sight. The shooter can then unwittingly load a 12 gauge on top, resulting in a very efficient pipe bomb! The same thing can occur with the 28 gauge and 20 gauge.

Finally, here is a true and actual situation that I reluctantly witnessed on a grouse moor on the Duke of Buccleuch's estate in Langholm. Once during a grouse shoot, the loader in the next grouse butt was peppered with shot from about 40 yards away. Seventeen pellets were removed from the unfortunate man's face, one less than inch above his right eye. Thankfully there was no permanent damage. But the alarming thing was the mistake was made by another gamekeeper with over 40 years' gun-handling experience under his belt. Surprising? Not really. Statistics prove that most mistakes are made by experienced bird hunters. The experienced hunter takes things for granted more so than the novice who has been briefed properly in safe gun-handling procedure. Always remember, safe shotgunning is no accident.

CHAPTER 2

The Devil's in the Dominance

I should recall to mind that there is at least one case on record where a man was diagnosed by try-gun fitting as having a left master eye, when in fact, the eye in question was made of glass.

—Gough Thomas Garwood

"Pete . . . telephone!" my wife Alison shouted from the back porch. It was early morning, and as usual, I was exercising our two dogs in the woods at the back of our property. I puffed quickly up the hill and reached the house.

"Guy enquiring about a lesson," Alison said as she handed the phone over and then added, "He sounds nice."

I introduced myself to the caller and after the usual exchange of pleasantries, posed a few questions to him as I always do and listened intently to his replies. By doing this, sometimes it's possible to glean a few clues to the nature of the problem.

"I'm a pretty good shot on quail," reported the client, and then he added, "but not much good on doves and ducks. We're going to Argentina next month, so I thought you might be able to help."

I confirmed that I thought I could, and we arranged to meet at my local shooting facility in a day or so.

Sure enough, when we met, I immediately felt as though my wife's intuitions had been correct, and Jeff appeared to be an affable guy. A few questions revealed that he had been a keen shotgunner and bird hunter for many years. Most of his life he had been an almost fanatical quail hunter, and he owned a desirable piece of property in West Texas but (as is often the case) seldom had the chance to use it as much as he would have liked. He had recently sold a software business and explained that now, with more time on his hands and more or less financially independent, he had every intention of aggressively pursuing his bird-hunting passions.

Jeff's gun of choice was a Browning Citori 20 gauge and a quick check revealed that it was a pretty good fit. We walked onto one of the skeet fields to see how he could shoot. First Jeff tried a few low house targets from station one. The targets were crushed convincingly. On station two, the result was the same; all the targets were hit. He wasn't quite as successful on station three but hit most of the targets. Next we moved to station seven to try the high house targets. He crushed high house seven convincingly, and I could sense that by now Jeff was secretly smug about his shooting because he missed very few targets.

"What do you need me for, Jeff?" I joked as we walked over to station six. I pulled the first target . . . and was surprised that he missed it cleanly. Then more surprises: out of the first six targets, only one was chipped. But at least now I had something to work with. It's difficult to suggest a solution to a problem if the client is breaking all the targets!

"No problem, Jeff," I consoled him. "Let's try station five." Six more targets, zero hits. By now, Jeff was understandably getting frustrated.

"See!" he exclaimed. "This is what happens. I don't understand it!" But I did, and I have witnessed similar situations on hundreds of occasions. Try as he might, Jeff could not convincingly connect with most of the targets that were coming from the left, especially the ones that needed some lead.

It is possible for a right-shouldered shooter with a left master eye to shoot reasonably well on narrow-angle targets because they require a very minimum lead requirement. Most quail fall into this category, as do all trap-type targets. Even with the shooter's off eye taking over as he triggers the shot, on these targets, the spread of the pattern at

this range may be approximately 30 inches wide. The actual lead requirement on a narrow-angle shot like this may only be a few inches, so the width of the ample pattern will be more than enough to compensate.

But as Jeff progressed to stations five and six, the lead requirement on this wider angle and full crossing increased also to several feet. In this case, the visual input that the brain receives is coming from the wrong eye, so he misses the target. This is known as cross firing.

"So what's the problem?" Jeff asked me.

"I'm pretty sure your left eye is taking over on the left-to-right shots," was my reply.

Jeff was wide-eyed. "Are you sure?" he asked, almost indignantly. "I know I'm strongly right-eye dominant." Unfortunately, Jeff's statement was incorrect for two reasons. First, he was sure that his right eye was strongly dominant. This is an incorrect assumption to make (I will explain more about this later). Second, he mistakenly thought (as so many shooters do) that eye dominance has something to do with eye strength. So what exactly is eye dominance and why can it affect our shotgunning so dramatically?

The crossover stock of yesteryear was the first solution for cross dominance.

Solving Dominance Problems

For centuries, shotgun shooters, coaches, and gun fitters have tried to find ways to prevent the wrong eye from taking over *as the gun comes into the shoulder and the shot is taken*. I put that in italics because it is possible for someone to test right-eye dominant, but as he mounts the gun, the left eye can take over as he triggers the shot. (The opposite can happen with someone who is left-eye dominant.) In *The Gun and Its Development*, possibly the most comprehensive and elaborate work ever written about firearms, W. W. Greener describes two solutions for cross dominance. The first is the crossover stock, in which the shotgun was severely bent over to the left so that the gun could be shot from the right shoulder by a shooter with a left master eye. I have seen and shot several of these guns, and many years ago when I owned a gun shop in Scotland, I was offered one for sale. At that time, I mistakenly thought that the asking price was too high, so I declined. It was a big mistake; today crossover stocks are a rarity and command a high price.

In my opinion, the main reason most shooters resorted to the crossover stock was because they had already shot for many years and become familiar with the muscle memory involved with shooting from the right shoulder. Another unique way to circumvent a cross-dominance problem is the Monopeian sight, which was a set of sights that attached to the barrels. They were set so that the left eye was peripherally positioned as the gun was pointed and point of aim was to the same place. The gun fitter or coach would then painstakingly regulate the point of aim on a pattern plate to suit the eyes and facial contours of the user.

Many other devices were developed later, such as John Pesket's Eye Corrector/Obliterator. He worked for gun makers Cogswell and Harrison. This company, founded in 1770 by Benjamin Cogswell, is London's oldest surviving gun maker. The Obliterator was simply a round patch that

The modern equivalent of the patch is the glow bead, which can only be seen when the correct master eye is in alignment.

clipped onto the barrels of the side-by-side. The shooter slid the patch forward or backward to adjust it so that when he mounted the gun, the patch was between his wrong eye and the muzzles. This meant that the right shoulder shooter could only see down the barrels with his right eye as he aimed the gun. Both eyes could be fully open, providing normal peripheral, binocular, and stereoscopic vision right up to the time he securely seated the gun in his shoulder pocket and triggered the shot.

Yet another ingenious invention was a shooting glove with a large patch sewn onto the side. As the gloved hand gripped the fore-end of the shotgun, the patch would prevent the shooter from looking down the barrels with the dominant but off-shoulder eye.

Today's modern equivalents of these cross fire eliminators are fiberoptic sights set in tubes. You can only see the glowing dot on the end of the barrel when the gun is mounted and your head is in the correct alignment with the gun stock. All these contraptions do basically the same thing—you must only be aware of the muzzles in your peripheral vision as you trigger the shot. It is impossible for the human eyes to focus on two things that are moving at different speeds in the same frame.

Eye Dominance Tests

There are several ways to test for eye dominance. Many years ago, I used a small camera. I left the camera on a table top and casually asked the client to quickly take a picture of something in the distance. This ploy usually worked; most times, the client never suspected that I was testing him for

dominance, and as he picked the camera up, he would move it unerringly to his master eye.

You can also point a finger at an object in the distance, first closing one eye and then the other to see which one remains in line with the object. In my experience, depending on the day and the stress level and nervousness of the shooter, this test can be hopelessly inconclusive.

Another way to test for dominance is to hold both hands palms outward, with a small opening between them, as in the photos to the right. Extend your arms fully, and then sight a distant object through the hole. (A rolled up piece of paper also works.) With the object visible in the hole, bring your hands back to your face to determine which eye has acquired the image.

Over the last thirty years or so, I have carried out this test with my students. Most of the time it works, but sometimes it doesn't. Sometimes clients deliberately try to influence which eye they choose for their master eye. In other words, if we use the outstretched hands method as an example, the hands move toward the left eye but then switch across to the right at the last second. For some reason, there is a stigma attached to left-eye dominance.

More articles have been written about the controversial subject of eye dominance than probably any other shooting topic . . . and why not? Our eyesight is the most complex of our senses. We become successful with a shotgun by converting visual information into physical movement, which will hopefully then put the gun in the correct place relative to the target. We may use our eyes to see, but our success with a shotgun depends on how well our brain interprets what we do with what we see. Our eyes and hands must work as a team to ensure that the gun is positioned correctly relative to each target. In short, we have two cam-

Sometimes you can use a camera to test for eye dominance. Most times, without thinking, the shooter will position the camera over his correct master eye.

Testing for dominance: Left master eye.

Right master eye.

eras on the front of our head that our brain relies on for this visual information, but only one of the cameras is positioned above the rib of the gun. If, because of a dominance miss-match, it's the wrong one, we will never shoot successfully.

MYTH: Right-eye dominant, right-shouldered shooters must keep both eyes open.

Over the years I have been a shooting coach, I have found that some of the information we are expected to believe is simply not true. So now is a good time to dispel some of these myths.

One of the most popular beliefs is that if we are diagnosed as right-eye dominant and we shoot from our right shoulder, we must keep both eyes open. Most shooting coaches will tell you this. This is absolutely not true for some of us.

Eye dominance is a neurological phenomenon, and it depends on how each eye is wired to the brain. When we become neurologically mature in young adulthood, some optic nerve hookups go to one side of our brain, some go to the other. If, for example, 80 percent of the hookups connect to the right side of the brain and the remaining 20 percent connect to the left, then you are right-eye dominant. It is possible that a shooter with such a strong dominance could shoot well with both eyes open. However, another shooter with 55 percent of the hookups connecting to the right side and 45 percent connecting to the left would still test right-eye dominant, but the dominance is so slight that the left eye could be persuaded to take over in some shooting situations. The dominance test may be correct, but the degree of dominance is less and may cause problems, which, in turn, may lead to cross firing.

Take note that we become neurologically mature in young adulthood. Sometimes the paths for young aspiring shotgunners are not clearly marked. A youngster at twelve years old may test as right-eye dominant and then two years later test conclusively left.

Try this at home. If you are a right-shouldered shotgunner, focus on a distant object and then

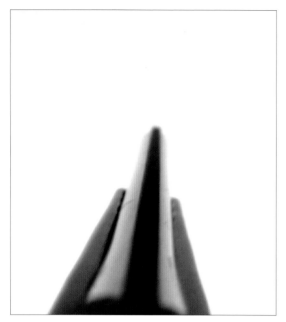

With strong dominance, you should see a clear image of the shotgun barrel in your periphery similar to this picture.

If the dominance is weak, or almost equal dominance, you may see a ghost image. This visual input is confusing for the brain. Both these pictures were taken with the camera above the barrels to illustrate the point.

point your right index finger at it. Do not look at your finger as you do this. Focus on the object in the distance, keeping the pointing finger in your peripheral vision. With both eyes open, you will see an image of two fingers instead of one: a bold image of your finger and also a ghost image. This is a phenomenon that optometrists call binocular disparity.

With strong right-eye dominance, the brain will select the bolder image (which should be the right one), but if the dominance is slight, you'll be confused about which of the images is the clearer. If you are to shoot successfully, you must always know where the barrel is relative to the target. In other words, you must see a clear, well-defined bird/barrel relationship. If you substitute the shotgun barrel for the finger, it will be difficult, as you bring the gun to point of aim, to define which image of the muzzles to use for the correct bird/barrel relationship. Closing the off eye will stop this.

MYTH: Some shooters never see the barrels when they shoot.

Here's another myth about seeing a bird/barrel relationship. Over the years I have had conversations with clients who, at first, swear emphatically that they never see their barrels when they shoot. How can they avoid seeing them, I wonder? The barrels are central to their line of vision.

Common sense should prevail here, but for many, it does not. Routine questioning of these clients, however, reveals the truth. For example, if I ask the client to focus on an object in the distance, a tree or utility pole, and ask him what he sees, his answer will be that he clearly sees the object in question. If I ask him to mount his shotgun and point it at the same object, and ask him what he sees now, his answer should be, "I see the object in hard focus, but I see my barrels in my peripheral vision." In other words, he does see his barrels, but he doesn't look at them. There is a difference. If he really doesn't see his barrel, how would he know how far in front of the target he was pointing the muzzles as he pulls the trigger? Without seeing the barrels, surely this would be the equivalent of attempting to shoot lightning bugs in pitch blackness.

British shooting expert and engineer Gough Thomas Garwood conducted experiments to prove that, regardless of what we may think, the subconscious view of the barrels definitely influences the pointability of the gun. In the experiments, with the aid of a spotlight projector down the barrel of his gun, in complete darkness in an unlit room, he fired twenty-five shots at a pinpoint of light on the wall. He then did twenty-five shots in daylight. He found out that his pointing ability was at least 50 percent better when he could see the barrels of the gun in his periphery. The conclusion that he came to was that although we may think we shoot instinctively with no awareness of the barrels, in practice this is not the case.

Today, an enterprising manufacturer has produced a light that slips down inside the barrel of a shotgun to aid and improve gun-mounting and gun-pointing technique. Anyone out there who still doubts that a peripheral view of his barrels is necessary for accurate pointability may carry out his own experiment (as I have done) with one of these lights. I think he would find the results interesting.

Cross Firing

Sometimes shooters object to closing an eye. In an effort to prove my point to some of them that cross firing was indeed occurring on some of their shots, I conducted an experiment. At the Dallas Gun Club, one of the target presentations on the sporting clay course was a full crossing shot at about twenty-yard range travelling just above the surface of a lake. The shooting station was an elevated platform at about 90 degrees to the flight line of the target. I always asked the clients to describe the target to me and evaluate it before they attempted to break it.

"What sort of target is this?" I asked.

"Full crossing shot, about twenty yards away, about three to four feet of lead," the client said.

"OK. Good. Let's see you shoot ten of them. Following pairs."

The client obliged. The first pair was usually crushed convincingly and possibly the second pair. Maybe also the third pair. But usually, if my suspicions were correct and cross firing was sometimes occurring, sooner or later, he would miss one of the targets. When this happened, the client was openmouthed.

"Can't understand why I missed that target, the lead looked exactly the same to me as the other shots."

Of course it did—the visual input to pull the trigger had been received by one of the eyes, but unfortunately on this occasion, it was the wrong one and the target was missed. But if the client doubted that cross firing was the reason for the miss, my next question proved that this was indeed the case, beyond reasonable doubt.

"So where did your shot pattern go?" I asked the client. It wasn't difficult to see.

"I shot about four feet in front of the target!" he exclaimed.

Exactly! Because we were shooting down at the target as it skimmed above the surface of the lake, it was plain to see by the pellets hitting the surface that the client's shot went in front of the target, proving that as the shot was triggered, his left eye was influencing the proceedings instead of his right.

Bird hunters, especially if they like to hunt ducks, can learn a lot from this. I did a lot of duck and goose hunting both in Scotland on the Solway Firth estuary in Dumfriesshire and Eagle Lake on the Katy Prairie near Houston. Shooting ducks over water can be an eye-opener for many of us, not just to identify an eye dominance problem that may manifest itself, but also to identify just how much lead we need on fast flying birds. With a low shot there is no mistake as the pellets strike water below the target. A high shot, due to a head lift, poor gun fit, and so on, is also plain to see, but usually, only on the close shots (up to 20 yards). Sometimes, as distance increases on these high shots, it's hard to see where the pellet distribution registers.

The dominant visual impression of side-by-side barrels.

The shooter's same view of an over-and-under shotgun. Now the dominant impression may be the two stacked barrels that the shooter's left eye sees. This is enough for the wrong eye to take over as the gun is brought to point of aim.

But the real eye-opener for most inexperienced shots is the lead requirement. Next time you are presented with a flock of mallards or greenheads skimming over the decoys, watch where a couple of shots from your buddies in the duck blind go and I bet you get a surprise. You can do the same exercise with doves that are dropping into a tank for a thirst quencher before they go to roost.

MYTH: You can train your nondominant eye to become the dominant one.

Another myth is that you can train the subdominant eye to take over and become the dominant one. Once again, simply not true. Depending on the degree of dominance, you can influence which eye takes over by sticking one of the increasingly popular glow beads on the end of your gun. There is nothing new in this. The old seasoned duck hunters would use chalk or a wax crayon to enhance the ribs on their shotguns so that they could see them better in the low-light conditions of early morning duck hunting forays.

The type of gun you use, even the type of rib on the gun, can influence which eye takes over as the gun is brought to point of aim. Many years ago I had a client who had shot well all his life with a side-by-side, but every time he tried to shoot an over-and-under, he would shoot down the left side of the target. An eye dominance test revealed that he was left-eye dominant, but the dominance must have been slight, almost central vision. The dominant visual impression, as he brought his side-by-side up to point of aim, was the one of the wide horizontal view of the barrels, which his right eye was receiving.

However, when he did the same with the over-and-under, the situation was the reverse and the dominant visual impression was the one that his left eye saw of the barrels because they were now stacked vertically. His left eye would take over, and he would shoot down the left side of the target every time. This is exactly the same reason that some shooters claim that a glow bead can cure a dominance mismatch. It can't; what the glow bead does is enhance the view of the barrels in the peripheral vision, which in turn gives the shooter a clearer indication of a bird/barrel relationship as he triggers the shot.

So what's the answer if you suspect an eye dominance problem? Experiment. Shoot with both eyes open and again with the off eye—the eye *not* above the rib—closed. Shoot also with a premounted gun to eliminate the possibility of a miss-mount.

Don't experiment out in the field with live quarry. The hardest part is deciding what a bird will do and when it will do it, so no two shots will be identical; your experiment would prove nothing. Instead shoot in a controlled environment such as a skeet field. Low house station two is ideal. Shoot four targets with both eyes open, and then the same target again with one eye closed.

You must also shoot with sustained lead because once again, changes in gun movement will give you inconsistent results and prove nothing. In other words, with a fast swing you may break the target, but with a slow swing you might not. Take note of how well the targets are breaking; with one eye they may be pulverized, two eyes they may be chippy, proving that the bird/barrel relationship you see is not as clear as it should be due to inconclusive (or weak) dominance. You may be surprised with the results.

One final thing. The nature of shotgunning is that everyone who likes to shoot a shotgun considers himself a shooting coach. Don't be misled by advice from others who say what they say just because everyone else says it. I have known shooters who have struggled for years to keep both eyes open because others tell them that it is the only way. Advice from others with dominance issues may not be the answer for you. We are individuals; none of the guys offering this (usually) free advice know what you see as you trigger the shot, only you do.

CHAPTER 3

Why Gun Fit and Gun Mount Are So Important

Any stock that in its back recoil or kick does not automatically relieve the pressure on the cheek is entirely bad. That is, it does not fit the shooter, and it will sooner or later make him afraid of the gun.

—*G. T. Teasdale-Buckell*

We often hear it said that we aim a rifle, but we point a shotgun. Very true. Successful use of a rifle depends on a rock steady aim as you line your eye up with the rear and front sight on the gun with a stationary object. With a shotgun, however, you are attempting to intercept something that is moving. You simply cannot focus on the end of the gun and the target at the same time; the human eye is incapable of doing this. This is why good gun fit is essential. As the gun is mounted to the shoulder, the master eye must be in perfect alignment with the rib, without checking this by looking at the gun. In other words, the shooter's eye becomes the back sight. A glance at the gun, however fleeting, spells disaster for the successful bird hunter. A premounted gun may work well for skeet and sporting clays, but live birds are different. Predictably unpredictable, we never know where they are coming from or going to. For any degree of success, our gun mount must be unerringly accurate, every time.

Misalignment by as little as a quarter of an inch at the shotgun end will translate into a miss of several feet at the target end. Let's say that as you shoulder the gun, your master eye is elevated above the rib by as much as a quarter of an inch. If you project a line down the rib of the gun out to the target to about 20 yards and another line out to the target from the pupil of the shooter's eye, that quarter-inch misalignment at the gun end translates into a miss several feet over the top at the target end.

One of the main reasons for missing live birds is lifting your head, even more so on descending birds. The reason is simple. If you bring the shotgun to your shoulder too early and the bird is coming down—a duck dropping into the decoys or a dove descending onto the sandy shoreline perimeter of a pond in the evening, for example—the gun may move to intercept the bird, but your face will stay where it is. In other words, your hands move the gun downward to intercept the bird, and this pulls the gun away from your face. Keeping the gun out of your shoulder until the shot is triggered will reduce the tendency for this to happen. It all comes down to good gun-mounting technique. If the mount is good, the gun will shoot where its user looks.

An even worse example of poor gun mounting causing problems in the field is the large bruise many get on their upper arms after a dove, duck, or pheasant hunting trip. The sudden appearance of the fast flushing bird triggers a physical response— we throw the gun up in a desperate attempt to get on him. Unfortunately, the butt of the gunstock often ends up nowhere near where it should be, but we trigger the shot anyway. The bruise shows that the gun is about four to six inches off from where it should be. Project two lines out to the target now, and the inevitable miss may be by several feet.

Perfecting Your Gun Mount

To perfect your gun mount, lift the gun into the shoulder pocket by using both arms in unison. Push the gun forward slightly with a bayoneting action and simultaneously lift the gun smoothly to the face and into the shoulder pocket with the combined movement of both arms. Don't raise the back hand first, allowing the gun to pivot around the front hand.

Chopping down on the target happens when your back hand lifts the stock and the muzzles dip, as in the photo on the next page. Many quail hunters mount the gun like this. On occasion, I have witnessed these guys, during a gun-fitting session on the pattern plate, miss the plate entirely because at the point of pulling the trigger, the muzzles dip down. An errant movement in the wrong direction, however momentary, is costly if the intended quarry is a fast-flushing bird that is flying upward. As you mount the gun, both arms should be working as a team. They must lift the gun in unison, with what I call a parallel action, and the gun will come smoothly onto the line of the bird.

The upland bird hunter can use this technique to perfect gun mount. Suspend a string from a doorframe or a beam in the garage. Tie a loop in the string so that the muzzles of your gun will slip into it at about 6 inches below eye level and then practice your mount again.

You will find that as the muzzles of the gun push forward to complete the mount, the muzzles will remain parallel with the ground and not dip down each time. Twenty or thirty mounts like this for a day or two will improve your consistency.

A slight lift of the head, by as little as a quarter of an inch, will translate into a miss of several feet over the target.

 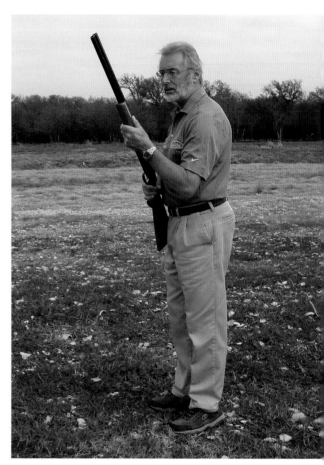

Left: The ready position. Here the gun is about 8 inches or so above my waist. *Right:* With the gun in this position, as your back hand lifts the stock, the muzzles will dip down.

Practice your gun mount until it becomes spontaneous, without the need for conscious thought. Each time you lift the gun, say to yourself just as you complete the mount, "into the gun." This will eventually make your mount more spontaneous, and most important, you will stay in the gun as you trigger the shot.

Webster's dictionary defines spontaneity as "acting or arising naturally and without constraint from an inner impulse, not planned or contrived." This is what we must do as the sudden appearance of the bird triggers a visual response. If the mount isn't spontaneous and we can see the bird for any length of time, many of us execute a gun mount that borders on time-consuming paralysis, culminating in a final head wiggle just to make sure we are looking down the rib. If this sounds like you, you have work to do. Don't forget, on some birds (quail and most fast-flushing birds, for example) there is very little time to waste.

When to Evaluate Gun Fit

Next time you visit your local gun shop, watch what happens when a prospective buyer selects a gun from the rack. My guess is that he will shoulder the gun up a few times, and then each time he does this, wriggle his head about so that his eye is more or less lined up with the bead.

"Ah yes," proclaims the observant shop assistant (who is more than likely on a healthy commission for selling him the gun in the first place), "that seems to be a good fit for you." Then he adds with a knowing wink, "Yes, sir. You'll put plenty of birds in the bag with that gun." Unfortunately, both the shop assistant and potential buyer have got it wrong.

If the potential buyer has been shooting for a few years and has acquired some shotgun technique, he may abandon the gun in favor of another from the rack that just feels better dynamically and mounts more correctly to his master eye. But even then, if the gun that he selects has nice engraving, or the stock has a nice piece of sexy-looking well-figured walnut, there is still a slim chance that the buyer will abandon objectivity. He will often slacken his purse strings and part with his cash for a gun that doesn't really fit in order to impress his shooting buddies.

Anyone can pick up any shotgun and make it conform to his personal physical dimensions by mounting it and then wriggling his head around. But, unfortunately, that does not mean that the gun is a good fit for him. In other words, the gun must be made to fit the user, not the other way around. New shooters don't understand this and try to use a shotgun like they would a rifle.

The following scenario is very common with the husband that selects a gun for his wife. Big-game hunting safaris are fashionable all across the US. Perhaps the husband and wife have enjoyed hunting plains game together with rifles on these safaris. Now the husband has decided that his wife, for the first time in her life, might like to learn to shoot winged game with a shotgun. The conversation in the gun shop might go something like this:

"My wife and I are going on a dove hunting trip to Argentina next month, and she needs a shotgun. I would also like her to use it for doves and quail. What would you suggest?"

The eyes of the gun shop assistant begin revolving like the numbers on a one-armed bandit in a Vegas casino.

"Ah, yes, sir, we have just what you are looking for," he replies, as he skillfully steers the happy couple toward the most expensive gun cabinet in

I tied a piece of string onto the top bar of a safety cage at my local gun club. I slipped the muzzles through this and practiced the gun mount. The string will prevent the seesawing action of the gun as it pivots around the front hand. The move to the target will be much quicker and more efficient as a result.

the store. Selecting a nice 20-gauge side-by-side from the dazzling array in the top shelf cabinet, he opens the gun and passes it to the husband. The elegant carved fences and gold inlay on the action are an instant attraction for the wife. The glowing, amber tones of the well-figured French walnut, graceful curves and the sweeping lines of the straight English stock add to the attraction. The husband passes the gun to his wife, and she attempts to mount it a few times.

"It feels so light," she squeals delightedly, "so much better than those heavy guns of yours, darling!"

The salesman smiles to himself in smug secrecy; he knows his stuff. He's seen it all before, and he knows the gun is as good as sold. A few more guns are picked from the shelf, equally nice guns, but (in the lady's eyes) none seem to compare with the first one.

"We'll take it," the husband says, his wife squeals with more delight, and the shop assistant pitches in with the next phase.

"Of course, sir," he says, "now we will need to make sure that the gun is a good fit for your wife."

He proceeds to show the lady how to mount the gun. Each time he does this, he stands in front and peers down the muzzles at her eye to make sure the gun is in the right place. Then he gently moves her head up and down or left and right to compensate if it isn't. In other words, he tries to get the lady to mold herself to the gun, not the other way around. Forget it. Moving your head after you mount the gun to produce the correct sight picture/bead alignment is a complete waste of time.

Our salesman-come-gun-fitter also makes impressive-looking notes on a fitting form of any alterations that must be made to the stock to make the gun fit. Don't forget that at this stage, the shooter has never handled, let alone fired, a shotgun. Fitting a shotgun to a new shooter in this way is a complete waste of time. In a month or two, when the lady has become proficient at mounting the gun and familiarized herself with the handling dynamics, she will need to return the gun to the store and have the stock rebent—unfortunately at the cost of another $1,000.

Many times over the last twenty years or so clients have come to me and asked me to teach their wives to shoot. Sometimes the gun the husband brings for his wife to use is a wise choice; it's a reasonable fit and it has some weight to it to keep recoil to a minimum. Other times, the gun is not a good choice, and I politely refuse. This, unfortunately, often upsets the husband, who may have parted with a small fortune for the gun, and he asks why I would refuse.

After three or four shots, the gun will be whacking the lady so hard in the face and shoulder that she'll be ready to abandon shotgunning and take up golf or tennis instead. And there is another reason I refuse. Months later, the same woman is at a sporting clay charity shoot. She hates using the gun with a passion now and couldn't care less if she hits anything or not with it . . . and it doesn't go unnoticed.

One of the onlookers at the event nudges his companions. "You see that lady over there? She couldn't hit a cow in the arse with a banjo!" Then he adds, "Didn't Pete Blakeley teach her to shoot?" So my credibility is on the line.

Several years ago, after being faced with this situation on numerous occasions, I visited one of the gun shops in the Dallas area. I politely asked one of the salesmen which shoulder he shot from and he said his right shoulder. I then asked him to select a gun from the rack and asked him if he would oblige me by mounting the gun instead on his left shoulder.

The sales assistant looked at me quizzically, but then did as I asked and mounted the gun. It was immediately obvious that this was very difficult for him to do. Try as he might, the gun just did not go where he intended it to. His head contorted all over the place, and he was wriggling for all he was worth to get the gun somewhere near the right place.

"It feels awkward," he eventually admitted.

"That," I said to the assistant, "is exactly how new shooters feel when they try to mount a shotgun for the first time."

I must have made an impression, because new clients started appearing with stocks with more or less standard dimensions and any alterations were made after their mounting technique improved, not before.

All shotgun manufacturers apply a set of standard stock dimensions to all off–the-shelf guns.

These dimensions are approximately 14$1/2$ inches length of pull, approximately 1$1/2$ inches drop at nose, and approximately 2$1/4$ inches drop at heel. There will most likely be a small amount of cast, $1/4$ inch at heel and slightly more at toe. The manufacturers know that these measurements will be acceptable for the average shooter. If the user is somewhere between the parameters of 5' 10" and 6' 2" and 170 to 200 pounds, the off–the-shelf gun may be a reasonable fit for him and point where he looks. But if he isn't . . .

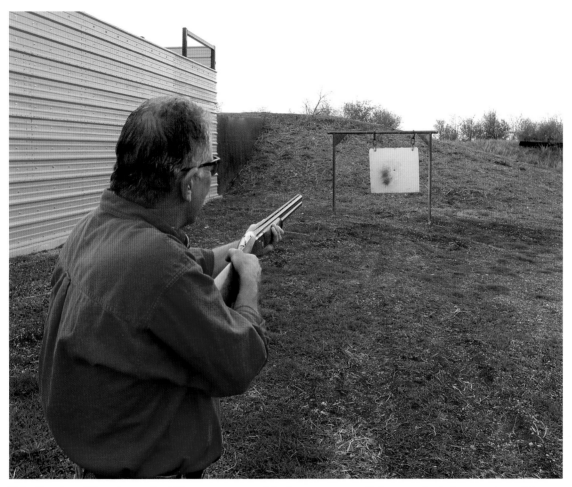

This client has diligently practiced his gun mount until he is spontaneous. Unfortunately, during a pattern plate session, the shot impact prints show that his gun is shooting low and left. This means that both the cast and the comb height need to be increased.

When I first came here from the UK in 1997, gun fitters were as scarce as rocking horse droppings. Now they are springing up all over the place, like flowers in a roadside ditch. Some are good, some are not so good, but make no mistake, there is money to be made in the gun-fitting industry. Most competitive shotgunners eventually opt for an adjustable comb and an adjustable butt plate on their guns. Now they can tweak the guns to their hearts' content. Some of these guys become paranoid about the fit of their guns, and after a bad day on the sporting clay course or skeet field, out comes the Allen wrenches and they bang away for an hour or two on the pattern plate, convinced that their poor score is a gun fit problem. It may well be.

Luckily most bird hunters don't go to this extreme, and it is unfashionable to have an adjustable comb or butt pad on a bird hunting gun. Perhaps before you order that very expensive pheasant, dove, or quail gun, you should rough out the measurements with a regular and inexpensive gun. Then after using it for a season, you can transfer the measurements to the custom gunstock, and they have a good chance of being more or less correct. Because if they're not, the bird hunter who painstakingly and lovingly selects that piece of Turkish walnut may have it carved to the wrong dimensions. If that's the case, all he has now is an expensive piece of firewood.

I fit lots of guns, and often, when clients visit me for the fittings, they bring several guns, all with different dimensions. Immediately, this is a problem. Providing the client's gun-mounting technique is good, we can then go to the pattern plate

For most hunting guns, this is the pattern distribution we are looking for.

FITTING CHART

Name _____   Date _____

Right Handed	
Left Handed	

Shooting Shoulder	Right	
	Left	

Master Eye	Right	
	Left	

Shoots with

Both eyes open	
Left eye closed	
Right eye closed	

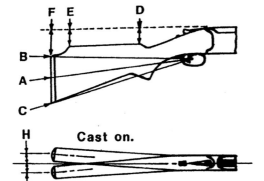

Grip Style

Straight
Swan neck
Pistol
Semi-Pistol
Prince of Wales

Cast on.

Cast off.

Length of Pull

A	To Centre	
B	To Heel	
C	To Toe	

Drop/Bend

D	To Comb	
E	To Monte	
F	To Heel	

Cast/Bump

G	To Heel	
	To Toe	

H	To Heel	
	To Toe	

Right Hand—Cast off

Left Hand—Cast on

_____

Remarks

This is a fitting chart that I use to note the dimensions of the client's gun.

to find out where the point of impact is for each gun. If the points of impact are different in each case, the guns need to be altered accordingly.

Over time, when we become competent shots, we build up a repertoire of bird/barrel relationships or sight pictures that we know to be correct. By using different guns that shoot to different points of impact, some of these bird/barrel relationships will not work for us, and we end up missing birds for no apparent reason.

If the first gun that the client shoots on the pattern board shoots with a perfect vertical alignment but the pattern is 100 percent high, he may have a degree of success and hit flushing, rising birds with

the gun. If the next gun he patterns shoots with a 60–40 percent pattern, he will shoot underneath those same birds. With a 60–40 pattern distribution, the user can keep the bird in view at all times above his barrels.

Length

There are four dimensions to consider when you fit a gun: length, drop, cast, and pitch. Length is also known as length of pull. It is measured from the center of the trigger (front trigger on a double gun) to the center of the butt plate. Most American guns come with a standard length of pull of

Length of pull must be measured in three places. With a side-by-side with a double trigger, these measurements must be taken from the front trigger.

This client is well over 6'6" tall, and this gun is far too short. As the gun recoils, his back hand on the grip will drive into his face and nose.

Holding a shotgun in this way so that the stock fits the crook of the arm and the finger reaches the trigger is not an acceptable way to determine length of pull.

about 14 to 14 1/4 inches. European guns are routinely slightly longer than this. A good gun fitter will measure length of pull from the trigger to the heel, center, and toe of the stock.

The widely used method of holding the gun at the grip with the trigger finger in position and seeing if the butt makes contact with the forearm is not a conclusive way to determine stock length.

Most shooting coaches will tell you that, when the gun is mounted, you should have at least one or two finger widths between the back of the hand and the front of the nose. This will depend on the position of the shooter's head on the stock.

With new shooters, where they place their heads will vary a lot until they learn to mount the gun correctly; this in turn may give the impression that the gun is too long initially. The stock should be as long as the user can comfortably mount and swing, so when new shooters are in the early stages of using a shotgun, don't be tempted to hack a lump off the end of the stock. As the users acquire some technique, they will mount the gun differently.

Here the try gun has been adjusted to give a much longer length of pull. This tall client needs a length of pull of about 15 1/2 inches. Any more than that and the gun may be difficult to mount with heavy clothing.

This is an adjustable gun that I use to determine the correct stock measurements. It adjusts for length, cast, drop, and pitch. The measurements are then taken with the drop gauge.

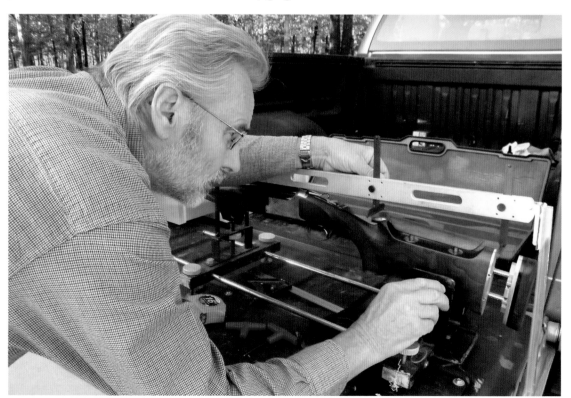

Taking an accurate set of measurements with the drop gauge.

Thickness of clothing must also be considered. A longer stock definitely does point and control recoil better, but if it is too long, it will catch on clothing and will be slow to mount. In other words, the 20 gauge with the 14-inch length of pull that is used for dove in South Texas may be fine when the user is wearing a thin shirt. But if the same gun is used in freezing conditions in the UK for driven partridge when the shooter now wears several layers of insulation, the extra clothing will increase the length of the stock to such an extent that as the gun is mounted, the shooter's eye will drop behind the receiver. The easiest way to remedy this is to fit a temporary comb raiser on the stock for cold-weather shooting.

A stock that is too short will cause bruising to the nose and face as the gun recoils. Also, in the final stage of the gun mount, muzzles of the short stocked gun may dip slightly. A happy medium, somewhere in between the long and the short, is what we are looking for.

Drop

Drop is arguably the most important measurement. If you place a straight edge along the top of the barrels, the measurement from the bottom edge of this to the top of the comb is known as the drop. There is a big variation, on a standard field stock, between the measurement at nose, which is the front of the comb, and at heel, which is the back.

Most field stocks have a standard drop at nose of $1^{1}/_{2}$ inches and $2^{1}/_{4}$ inches drop at heel. This makes the angle of the comb in relation to where the cheek touches it quite steep. Because of this relatively steep angle of a gun with a stock of these dimensions, the placement of the eye above the rib will vary accordingly depending on where the shooter places his head. This is explained in more detail later in this section. Although the gun may be perfectly acceptable to a shooter of average proportions, it will shoot low for someone who needs a short length of pull and high for someone needing a long length of pull. Any alteration to comb height will influence the position of the shooter's eye above the rib. The gun will shoot high, if the shooter's eye is too high. The shots will be low, if his eye is too low. If the shooter's eye is so low that it is hidden behind the breech, this will persuade the wrong eye to take over as the gun is brought to point of aim.

With a properly fitted gun, the butt pad as a whole should fit comfortably into the shoulder, and the heel should be level with or just below the top of the shooter's shoulder. If it isn't, as the gun recoils 100 percent of the recoil will be transferred to 50 percent of the shoulder pocket.

A point worth mentioning here is that a shooter with a long neck and sloping shoulders who favors side-by-side shotguns always feels some discomfort as the gun recoils, especially with a light gun and heavy shells. This is because she

The more rib you see, the higher the gun will shoot. The ideal position for the pupil of the shooter's eye is the second from the right.

Women routinely have longer necks than men. Most of the butt of this shotgun is above the woman's shoulder.

With some gun-mounting practice, and by adding a temporary comb raiser, the butt of the gun is where it should be.

may need such a large amount of drop that the resulting increased angle to the top of the comb will push the gun rearwards into her cheekbone. This is usually the main reason for bruising underneath the cheekbone.

The place where the face actually comes into contact should be marked when the stock is measured. I fit lots of guns to lots of clients, and during the fitting session, I stick a white paper label onto the top of the comb of the try gun. I put a mark in the center of this label and then a corresponding one on the client's face. Sometimes, as the client mounts the gun there will be a variation of up to 2 inches between each mount. In other words, the client may creep the stock on the first mount and be in front of the mark, level with the mark on the second, and behind the mark on the third mount. If we measure these differences with a drop gauge, the variable position of the client's eye will give a variable horizontal reading on the pattern plate. The skilled gun fitter should be able to estimate which measurement he needs for the correct fit.

Many competition shooters favor a Monte Carlo comb that is parallel to the line of the top rib. This means that regardless of the length of pull,

The position of the client's face should be marked on the label to determine the drop-at-face measurement.

Fitting for the female form. After a few shots, this woman will feel some discomfort as the toe of the shotgun digs into the top of her chest. A stock that has fairly large cast to offset the butt of the gun will prevent this.

the eye remains in the correct position. Most competition guns now have the luxury of an adjustable comb, and this makes sense because as our bodies change, our stock prescription changes too. Weight loss or gain and changes in flexibility due to age or injury can affect the way we bring the gun to point of aim. Many women also will benefit from a parallel comb simply because they routinely have longer necks than men do. Long-necked ladies have a habit of dropping their faces forward onto the stock as they complete the gun mount, and the parallel comb can compensate for this. Unfortunately, most traditionalists consider that a parallel comb on a game gun, especially an elegant English side-by-side, looks out of place. Because of this, they are rarely seen on double field guns, but they are popular with female shooters on semiautomatics.

Cast

Cast is the amount of deviation of the butt laterally from the line extended along the rib of the gun to give proper eye placement above the rib.

Cast is measured at heel and also at toe. When the shooter is a large-chested man with pronounced pectoral muscles, or a well-endowed woman, a stock with a pronounced toe will dig into the flesh of the shoulder pocket in the wrong area and cant the gun over at an angle as the gun recoils. The shot will be off to the side, if this happens, and there will be poor recovery for a second shot.

A stock angled to the right is known as cast off and one angled to the left is known as cast on. As a general rule, broad-shouldered people will require more cast than slightly built people. Any alteration to the cast of a gun will move the center of gravity, and depending on the gun type, the gun may then side flip, or pull to one side, especially if the choke barrel is fired. Finely built sides-by-sides with a small grip radius are extremely susceptible to this.

Years ago eye dominance problems were sometimes rectified by means of a crossover stock (see page 11), which greatly increased the side flip effect further. Two clients of mine who shot with these guns when I lived in the UK had problems with them. I am sure that with regular use, the user can subconsciously control this side flip, depending on which way the gun is swinging at the time the trigger is pulled. A gun should be brought smoothly to the face with the head erect, not canted over. Shooters often cant their heads sideways to make up for lack of cast, but it can cause bruising to the side of the face.

Pitch

Pitch is basically the way in which the gun fits the shooter's shoulder and the angle of the butt of the gun relative to the axis of the bore. Most guns have some down pitch, which is easy to measure by placing the butt of the gun squarely on the floor next to a wall and then sliding the gun toward the wall until the receiver touches it. The measurement between the muzzles and the wall is the pitch measurement.

Small pitch adjustments can dramatically influence the way recoil is transmitted to the shoulder. Too much down pitch and the butt will slide up during recoil, whacking the shooter under the cheekbone. Too little and the gun will slide down, producing excessive muzzle flip and shooting high.

Pitch and cast adjustments must complement each other. Just as with cast adjustment, a shooter with large pectoral muscles (or a well-endowed woman) will benefit from careful consideration to

Measuring down pitch on a shotgun gun by placing the butt of the gun on the floor. The farther the muzzles are away from the wall, the greater the down pitch.

pitch adjustment. Failure to do this will mean that the butt plate is in contact with only a small area of the shoulder pocket, and recoil is transferred to part of the pocket instead of the whole. If this main area of contact is the toe of the butt plate, once again, this can have painful consequences for the shooter.

If the shooter's shoulders are fairly narrow but he has large pectoral muscles, a recoil pad fixed at an angle will be an advantage. The heel of the pad should be in the shoulder pocket and the toe slightly further out toward the armpit. This is a comfortable solution for many people.

If, as your gun recoils, it whacks you under the cheekbone, suspect a pitch problem. Try this to prove it: Partially unscrew the two screws that hold the butt pad on the stock of the gun. Slide a quarter under the toe of the gun and retighten the screws. Is the recoil better or worse? If it seems better, slide another quarter under and shoot the gun again. If it is worse, slide the quarter between the stock and the heel of the gun, and do the same again. Doing this will increase or decrease the pitch so that eventually the entire surface of the butt fits snugly into your shoulder pocket. The pitch can then be measured from the trigger at heel, center, and toe, and a competent gunsmith can make a permanent fix.

Your Gun's Fore-End

Something else you should consider (but most shooters don't) is the fore-end of the gun. The front hand does the pointing, so it seems logical that if the shape of the fore-end can influence the way the gun assists this pointing attitude in the hands of its user, so much the better. Fore-ends come in many different styles. The splinter is found on all traditional English side-by-sides and is designed to be held in conjunction with the barrels. The disadvantage is that in situations where multiple shots are fired, the barrels quickly become too hot to hold—a serious problem on the productive driven pheasant shoot. The answer is

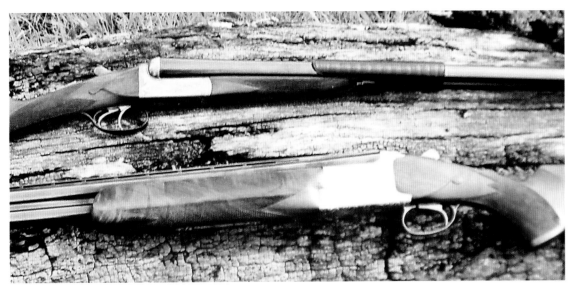

The comparison of the length of the fore-end can clearly be seen on these two guns. The splinter fore-end on the side-by-side requires a leather hand guard to protect the hand from the hot barrels.

the leather hand guard, but I have often seen some blistered fingers and heard some choice obsceni-ties when for some reason this essential piece of equipment was omitted.

The beaver tail is another style of fore-end on a side-by-side. The only gun I saw a beaver tail on in the UK was the Winchester Model 23 and the AYA No. 3.

Over-and-unders routinely have a bulkier fore-end. The semi–beaver tail and Schnabel or tulip are found on many over-and-unders. The hunting standard is slightly slimmer, without the beak of the Schnabel. The semi–beaver tail is found on many skeet and trap guns, and the full over-and-under beaver is in my opinion a real handful, and I have only ever seen it on two guns, both of which were made for the American market.

How Gun Fit and Gun Mount Work Together

A correctly fitted shotgun inspires confidence; the shooter gets subconscious, tactile assurance that tells him his head is in the right position as he triggers each shot. If, as you get dressed in the morning, you put your shoes on the wrong feet, you would realize there was a problem with the first steps you take. A perfectly fitted gun is the same, it just feels right.

Many coaches suggest that you practice your gun-mounting technique in front of a mirror, but be careful doing that. Sometimes it encourages consciously lining your eye up with the bead, which may be a bad habit to break when out in the field. In other words, as you complete each mount, you will quickly check that your eye is in alignment with the rib. Do this for a split second as you trigger a shot at live quarry in the field, and the gun will stop.

A much better way is to diligently practice your gun-mounting technique to acquire muscle memory, and then close both your eyes and mount the gun again. When you open them, your eye should be exactly down the rib. If your gun has a small center bead in addition to the end bead, as you open your eyes these two beads should be aligned, and as a general rule of

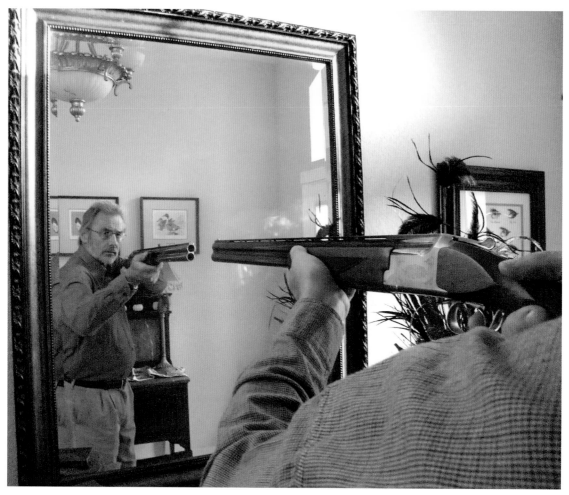

Some shooting coaches suggest perfecting your mount in front of a mirror. This can encourage a split-second glance at the gun to check alignment, so beware. A fleeting glance at the gun spells disaster.

thumb, these beads should be stacked like a figure eight. If the rib is ramping away from you and you can see a lot of it, chances are the comb is too high.

If as you open your eyes, it's obvious that the fit is less than perfect, alterations must be made so that it is. No cheating and no rationalizing! You want tactile assurance that the gun is in the correct place, not visual assurance by glancing at the rib to check alignment. You can peer down the barrel in front of the mirror as much as you like, but this still doesn't tell you where the gun shoots. The final evaluation of the gun in the hands of its owner is specific to each owner and can only be positively identified on a pattern board.

I can't emphasize enough that to achieve the proper gun fit, you must have the perfect gun mount. If you are positive that your gun mount is as near to perfect as you can get, try some shots at the pattern plate. A session on a pattern plate with an experienced gun fitter will expose a multitude of sins.

The Pattern Plate

The pattern plate is a thick steel plate about four feet square, the center of which is about four feet from the ground. There is a central mark, or target. Years ago, whitewash was brushed onto the plate to indicate the pellet strikes, but the problem with whitewash was that in cold weather it freezes, and it also washes off and dries. I concocted my own formula for pattern plate whitener, a mixture of titanium dioxide and canola oil, and now many shooting clubs throughout the US use it. Titanium dioxide is white paint pigment, and you can buy a small tin at either Lowe's or Home Depot. Mix a small cup of the pigment with six cups of the cooking oil and apply it to the plate with a roller. The mixture looks exactly like paint, but it never dries, never freezes, and doesn't wash off.

Today, you can find many demonstrations on Youtube that show how to pattern a shotgun. One of the most popular clips is the one where the guy demonstrating is bench-resting the shotgun, exactly like you would do with a rifle. Unfortunately, although this will prove the point of impact prints on the plate, it proves absolutely nothing in terms of gun fit for the individual as he uses the gun because by doing it this way, the result is a perfect pattern every time. Anybody can pick up any shotgun, and by wriggling his head about to position his eye correctly relative to the bead, shoot perfect patterns with the gun.

This is the correct way to use a pattern plate: Stand about sixteen yards from the board and focus only on the target area in the center. In other words, do not look at the rib or the bead on the end of the gun. Mount and lower the gun twice, and on the third mount, as you complete the mount and the gun comes into your face and shoulder, fire. No matter how tempting it may be

to do this, do not, under any circumstances, aim the gun like a rifle. I cannot stress how important this is, and many of us, under the scrutiny of the trained eye of an experienced gun fitter, will attempt to cheat and consciously line our eyes up with the bead.

If you attempt to use the shotgun like you would a rifle, you achieve nothing. If, after a few shots, the pattern placement is erratic, you have a gun-mounting problem. Go back to practicing your gun mount before you pattern the shotgun again.

If, however, after five or six shots, an area shows on the plate where the bulk of the shot is concentrated, now you can make adjustments to your stock to center the pattern. For every inch that the pattern is off target, the stock will need to be adjusted by $1/16$ inch. If the main shot concentration is 4 inches high and 4 inches left, for example, the stock needs $1/4$ inch more cast and $1/4$ inch needs to be removed from the comb height. Just like a tailor fitting a new suit, several visits to this stocker may be required until the stock is a perfect fit for the user.

The pattern plate is a steel plate with an aiming mark in the center.

The wood of the gunstock can be bent by applying heat. There are several ways to do this. Years ago the usual method was to pour hot linseed oil over the wrist of the stock until it became pliable. Modern alternatives to this include infrared lamps and hair dryers, but most stock alterations are best left to the expert. Elegant side-by-sides especially require an expert gun fitter because some older ones may have been repaired at the wrist and these repairs may not be apparent to the layman. Usually, the experienced stocker will thoroughly examine the area of the stock where the bend is to be made. If the stock has been repaired at some time, applying heat will soften the glue in this area and may destroy a quality gunstock.

Ideal shot distribution is 60 percent above the target and 40 percent below unless you favor a high-shooting gun. Many competitive trap shooters, for example, favor a gun that shoots high because in the initial stages of flight the targets are always rising. This means that the competitor can maintain visual contact with the target and still

Shot patterns like these expose poor gun-mounting technique.

Expert stocker Paul Hodgins from Utah puts the finishing touches on the measurements of a quality side-by-side by using a bending jig/setting table.

see the rising bird as he triggers the shot. A gun for shooting flushing birds might also need to shoot high for the same reason. But for bird hunting, all your shotguns should shoot to the same point of aim. In the heat of the moment, you can't consciously calculate depending on which gun you are using at the time. For example, a high-shooting gun may be perfect for putting a few extra rising quail in your bag but hopelessly inadequate for doves dropping into the tank in the evening for a sundowner because you will shoot over the top of them.

Personal Preference

The final evaluation of the shotgun in the hands of its user is particular to each shooter. Regardless of his personal requirements, he should make it his business to find out exactly where his gun shoots, and he must do this on a pattern board. A few shots at the pattern board can reveal a multitude of sins to the trained eye, and if it's done right, pattern board evaluation will make a big difference. Only then will the gun shoot to point of aim and those frustrating whiffs be transformed into confident hits.

If you pick up several different shotgunning books and read the recommendations for a dove gun, one book will tell you a 20-gauge over-and-under is the gun to go with. The next book will suggest a 12-gauge semiauto. Another book will tell you that you need a 12-gauge automatic for grouse and another will insist the best gun is a short-barreled side-by-side.

Which are the correct choices? The answer is all of the above and none of the above. Apart from some obvious restrictions with gun choice, it is largely a personal thing. You would not, for example, go quail hunting with a 9-pound competition 12-gauge K80, but more than once over the years I have come across a client or two who seemed to abandon logic and go with unacceptable options, like the client who insisted he would shoot a side-by-side .410 on stratospheric pheasants coming off the side of a Scottish mountain and the guy with the 12-gauge autoloader spewing out a full ounce and a quarter of shot at bobwhite quail.

Most upland birds can be hunted successfully with a 20 gauge. For waterfowl and perhaps pheasants, a 12 gauge would be perfect. Cheap guns are rarely a bargain. The market leaders for a reasonably priced, reliable shotgun are Browning and Beretta. Other cheaper guns come and go periodically, but these two, in my opinion, have stood the test of time. One good gun that fits its user like a proverbial glove will, just like his hunting dog, become his faithful companion and last him a lifetime. He will have confidence in it and feel comfortable when using it.

At the end of each chapter on particular birds, I give my personal preferences for guns, but these are my preferences; there simply is no hard-and-fast orthodoxy where field guns are concerned. Everyone is free to follow his own tastes and personal preferences to find a gun that he feels comfortable with. Only one thing is certain: The gun must fit its user, no exceptions.

CHAPTER 4

Muzzle Control

I have a very strict gun control policy: if there
is a gun around, I want to be in control of it.

—*Clint Eastwood*

For bird hunting, good muzzle control is one of the most important things to learn. Shotguns are dynamic. You must move them with absolute precision onto and along the flight line of the bird. This is called developing the line. If you can develop the line, you have a 50 percent chance of connecting. You cannot miss the bird above or below; you can only miss in front or behind. Your ability to do this efficiently is far more important in bird hunting than any other shooting sport.

Strictly speaking, in bird hunting, muzzle control and gun-mounting technique are one and the same; they cannot be separated. Think of it this way: In trap, skeet, and sporting clays, you are allowed to shoot with a premounted gun. Knowing when the target will appear, where it comes from, and where it eventually goes is a massive advantage, because most times, the trajectory of each target will be similar. With birds, the hardest thing is deciding what they are going to do and when they are going to do it, and they never do the same thing twice.

Of course many bird hunters shoot low gun skeet to hone their bird hunting skills, and this does help. Low gun skeet can help to hone your mechanical skills for bird hunting. But the advantage of more predictable targets on the skeet field still remains.

Providing you have reasonable eyesight and normal muscular coordination, moving the gun with controlled precision should be easy, but we all neglect it. With a new shooter, I always pull them a few low house targets on a skeet field and ask them to simply point at each target with an extended finger.

Pointing a finger is usually unerringly accurate; shooters follow the target from where they first see it as it exits the low house widow all the way to the ground. I then ask them to do exactly the same thing again, but this time with a simple pointer, like a pen or pencil. Once again, the point is accurate. This is hand-eye coordination at its best and is fairly straightforward. So far so good. Then I substitute the client's shotgun for the pointer and ask him to do the same again. Now the gun waves about all over the place, nowhere near tracing the true trajectory of the target, not even close. There are several reasons for this.

First and foremost, the student rarely, if ever, finds it necessary to attempt to glance back at his finger when he is pointing. He simply points it at the target, and his hand-eye coordination obliges. But as soon as the gun is substituted, many students have an overwhelming desire to look at the end of the gun just to make sure it is travelling along the true target trajectory. This is unnecessary, and I'll explain why.

When using any intermediary, we must have confidence in it. Does the tennis player eye the ball as he returns it over the net, or does he eye the end of the racket? Of course, he eyes the ball. Does the carpenter eye the head of the nail or the end of his hammer as he drives the nail into the timber? Of course, he eyes the nail. But neither of those two intermediaries, the tennis racket or the

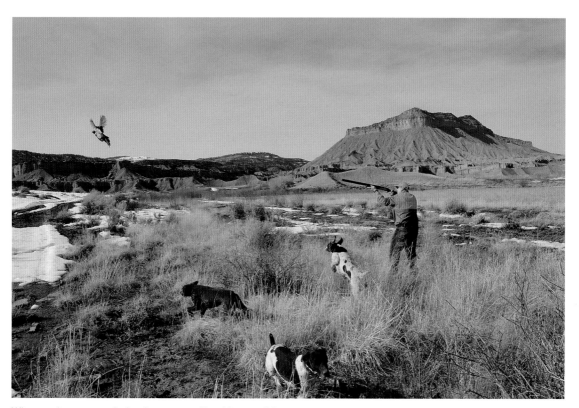

When a pheasant explodes from cover like this one did, you must react spontaneously to move and mount the gun with unerring accuracy. CASTLE VALLEY OUTDOORS PHOTO

A shotgun is an extension of your arm. It should conform to your natural ability to point.

hammer, are central to your line of vision like the muzzles of a shotgun barrels are. Until a new shooter really believes that if his gun fits, he doesn't need the backward glance at the muzzles or bead, he may shift focus to the end of his shotgun. It's called subconscious bead fixation, and it is very common.

Second, he is now using an intermediary that is a heavy shotgun. If the gun is a poor match for his physical capabilities, it will not respond as smoothly as his finger does. If the gun is too heavy for its user, it will more than likely start with a jerk, mak-

ing it difficult to trace the flight line of the target (or bird) accurately. This is known as forward inertia, and the gun will have the tendency to stray off line. But if the gun is a reasonable fit, and of suitable dynamics, it should respond perfectly well to the user's pointing ability just as naturally as pointing a finger. With a suitable gun, accurate line development should be fairly straightforward for the user.

Third, the gun is brought to the shoulder pocket too early. Most bird hunters use a two-part gun mount as they shoulder the gun. They see the fast-approaching bird, quickly mount the gun, and then with the gun already in their shoulder pocket, track the bird for too long. This is known as "boxing the bird," and it also leads the shooter to measure between the end of the gun and the bird, and in doing so, the shooter's eyes will alternate from the end of the gun to the bird. The swing along the bird's flight path will not be smooth, and the muzzle will stutter erratically as the target is chased along the trajectory.

Also, because we have two legs, the human torso pivots easily on a horizontal plane, rather like a tank turret. The human body always takes the easiest way to move. If the shooter uses the two-part gun movement, as soon as the butt of the gun is in his shoulder pocket, the muzzles will move horizontally relative to the target. Think about the ball player as he hits the baseball. As soon as he swings his bat and produces some momentum, the bat will prescribe a straight line as it cuts through the air. The same thing can occur with a shotgun. Because of the momentum produced, it will move in a straight line, and birds don't fly in straight lines. This problem is known as "dropping off line."

That dove or duck that approaches from the horizon seems to take forever to get here, doesn't it? For most shooters, the approach of the bird instills a feeling of panic, and they feel the need to mount the gun early just to make sure they have a good chance of getting on him. It's a mistake.

Mounting the gun early means that it is now central (and therefore partially obstructing) their line of vision. Because of this, their view of the quarry is restricted and any subtle nuance in the flight line may be unnoticed. Would you do the same when pointing your finger? I doubt it.

Visualizing a clock face can help you develop the line. This method is well established with my students, and once they become familiar with it, it's easy to implement. You always imagine the bird in the center of the clock and the approximate line he flies along corresponds to one the numbers around the face. It helps. I cover this in more detail in both the unit lead section and the driven bird section. The unit lead method that I developed is an easy way to indicate how much lead you need on a bird. It works very well.

For those of you who haven't tried it, low gun skeet is great practice for honing bird hunting mounting procedure. Next time you are near a skeet field, try this. Without calling for the target, stand on station one and get a shooting companion to pull a low house target. Count how many seconds it takes between the time you see it and the time it reaches your shooting position. It should take about three seconds. Providing your gun-mounting technique is good, three seconds is plenty of time to get on the bird. Even with fast-flushing birds, quail, walked-up pheasants, and grouse, you have a lot more time than you think, if you learn to shoot rhythmically. More about this later.

For bird hunting, the mount and swing should be a single, coordinated movement, not two separate movements. I can't emphasize enough just how important this is, especially in bird hunting situations. The gun must move just as efficiently as the outstretched finger. In other words, there should be no place where the mount ends and the swing begins.

This hunter has the gun too far from his shoulder, even though he can see these birds for a long time.

Perfecting Your Mounting Technique

The power to drive the gun is a combination of legs, thighs, hips, and upper torso. The butt of the gun should not come into the shoulder pocket until the shot is triggered. Within reason, the distance the gun is from the shoulder is directly proportional to the amount of movement you will need on that particular target. Obviously, if the quarry is quail or some other fast-flushing birds over dogs, you know the bird is imminent, so the butt of the gun will be positioned just out of the shoulder.

With a shot at a dove, pheasant, duck, or similar bird, when these birds can be seen approaching from a distance, the butt of the gun should be further from the shoulder but not too far. If the birds

can be seen for a long time, many shooters watch their approach with the gun positioned well down below their waist.

Mounting the gun from the position in the picture is too remote; the long trip for the gun from below the waist to its eventual position in the shoulder pocket causes the shooter to rush. Rushing ruins rhythm. Smoothness of line development is synonymous with economy of movement as the gun comes into the shoulder. It would make sense to use a more effective ready position that minimizes the distance of travel for these types of shots.

The correct position is somewhere between just out of the shoulder pocket (for fast-flushing birds) and slightly above the waist, where the bottom of the right elbow is just slightly above the waist line. With the gun in this position, you can make a smooth and economical movement onto the line of the bird without undue rushing. Remember the three Rs: Rushing ruins rhythm! By getting into the correct position, you'll have better visual contact with the target, and the shot will be more rhythmical. I cover this in more detail in chapter 7.

Most bird hunters have never done this before and find it difficult in the early stages, but once this technique has been mastered, it works very well. The reason it works is simple. If I ask a client to trace the trajectory of a target with an outstretched finger, he can do it with ease. If I then ask the client to do the same again, this time by keeping his outstretched arm and finger locked in one position and thus relying on moving his body to move his outstretched finger onto the line of the target, he will find it much more difficult.

Hand Position

The position of the shooter's hands can influence how the gun moves. The shotgun is an extension of your arms and must be pointed accurately. The muzzles must merge onto the line of the target

A shotgun should conform to your natural pointing ability. Some shooters prefer to extend the index finger of their front hand to complement this.

similar to the way we merge onto the freeway. The front hand is the controlling hand for the muzzles, and in fact many competitive shotgunners extend their index finger down the forearm of the gun to allow them to point the gun more effectively.

If your hand is positioned too far forward on the fore-end, it will restrict this movement as you develop the line. The correct way to determine where your front hand should be placed on the fore-end is as follows. Hold the gun with the trigger hand only and point it vertically. Raise the left arm and reach up to grasp the fore-end without undue stretching.

You want a comfortable fore-end position with your forearm bent slightly. The vertical gun position is the maximum the gun needs to move in any situation with overhead shots, so the front hand will also be positioned comfortably and enable you to control the gun efficiently in other situations requiring less movement. In situations when you need to make multiple overhead shots (a full day of driven pheasant or partridge, for example), you can move your forearm back slightly to allow for greater flexibility and comfort when making these shots. Without doing this (especially with driven pheasants), movement may be compromised, and you may pull the gun off line.

Also take a look at the position of your back hand. If your right arm is locked down tightly against your torso, your shoulder pocket will not be wide enough to accommodate the gun easily. This can cause a bruise on the upper arm.

Right to left crossing bird. In this position, my arm is held too close to my body and the shoulder pocket is almost nonexistent.

Determine where to place your hand by pointing the gun upward and then reaching up to comfortably grasp the fore-end with your front hand.

Here my elbow is at approximately 45 degrees to the horizontal and my shoulder pocket open.

With the gun in this position for a right-shouldered shooter, a shot at a right-to-left target means that, as you take the shot, the gun lies across the shoulder pocket, not firmly in it. If you get a bruise on the top of your arm, this is usually why. To avoid this, during the mount elevate your right elbow at an approximate angle of 45 degrees from the horizontal to open up the surface area of your shoulder pocket and relax the pectoral muscle to accommodate the butt of the gun easier.

Some trap shooters use an exaggerated high elbow position with their forearms parallel to the ground. They do this because it locks their cheeks into the gun.

Your Gun's Handling Dynamics

An accurate move to the target is also influenced by the gun's handling dynamics. The shotgun is a weapon of movement, and there must be a reactive relationship between the user, his gun of choice, and the quarry for which he intends to use it. Many shooters talk about balance in a shotgun, but balance is, to a large extent, immaterial. In the gun shop, some shooters hold a finger under the hinge pin of the gun and declare that, because the weight is equally distributed fore and aft, the gun will be perfect as an upland game gun. Where fast-flushing birds are the quarry, there is no doubt that the fast-handling gun may be an advantage, but to presume that is because such an ideal gun is lightweight and also balances at the hinge pin is, I'm afraid, a mistake. The heavier the gun is, the further back the balance point needs to be to make the gun feel lively.

Perhaps the easiest way to describe how the weight of a shotgun is distributed (covered in my book *Successful Shotgunning*) and how it affects your ability to swing it is as follows. Imagine a 4-foot long metal bar with two 3-pound weights that can slide up and down the length of it. If you grasp the bar in the middle and slide the weights in toward the center, the bar will be quick to start

(called the moment of inertia) and also quick to stop. Now slide the weights out to each end, and the bar (as you rotate it) will be slow to start and slow to stop. The overall weight of the gun will influence the directional maneuverability of the gun, but the way this weight is distributed will influence the rotational quality.

How well a particular gun handles in the hands of its user will depend on many factors, including the way the weight is distributed, the position of the user's hand on the fore-end, the type of backhand grip on the shotgun (straight English or pistol), and the relative strength of each of the user's arms.

The right-handed, right-shouldered guy may feel that a shotgun with a slight weight-forward bias responds perfectly for him in the field, but he may feel that he overpowers another gun of exactly the same overall weight because the weight is distributed equally in both directions fore and aft of the hinge pin. The reason for the difference is often that his right arm muscles are considerably stronger than his left. This is the same reason why some shooters, after surgery to fix a rotator cuff or tennis elbow, suddenly feel less at ease with their old faithful field gun. The ideal balance point is individualized.

If a shotgun has more weight toward the rear of the hinge pin, it will feel as though it points and handles faster than the gun that is muzzle heavy. If the user's forehand is just in front of the hinge pin (as it would be when holding most side-by-sides with splinter fore-ends), the gun will also feel lighter. The muzzle-heavy gun swings much smoother, and the felt recoil is usually less. The gun that is too heavy for the physical capabilities of its user will start with a jerk. This is known as forward inertia.

Ultimately, the handling dynamics of a gun are particular to each shooter. But with a new shotgunner, this will not be readily apparent. It may take many years of trial and error with multiple guns until he finds one that feels right. Most of us will favor a fast-handling gun for upland game, (like a side-by-side) and a slow and steady, weight-forward one (like a Benelli autoloader) for duck hunting. Note that I say most of us, not all of us, because eventually with experience, the dynamics and tactile qualities of a gun will appeal perfectly to its user for the purpose he intends it. And at the end of the day, that's all that really matters.

This shooter is practicing for his duck hunting trips. The targets are randomly released from the high or low houses on a skeet field without calling for them.

Skeet Field Practice

So what is the best way to hone muzzle control skills? In my opinion, the skeet field is ideal. The skeet field will teach you how to move the gun efficiently and also evaluate angles. The game of skeet was originated by two enterprising bird hunters in the 1920s as a way to hone their hunting skills in the close season. The two houses (high and low) on a skeet field are 40 yards apart. The center stake—the crossing point of the targets from the high and low houses—is about 20 yards (21 yards to be exact) from the semicircular walkway. Skeet targets travel at approximately 45 to 50 miles an hour. Guess what? So do a lot of game birds. You can shoot low gun skeet and also have someone pull the targets when you're not expecting them. (See chapter 7 for more.) Nobody will ever convince me that someone who is a good shot on the skeet field can be a bad shot in the field.

I take skeet practice a step further, mainly with my dove and duck hunting clients. After they have had a few shooting lessons, I sit them on a chair in any of the stations on a skeet field. I then pull targets when they least expect it. The effect at first is quite comical as they attempt to get on the bird and rise from the chair at the same time.

"Wait a minute! I wasn't ready for that one!" they shout indignantly.

Well, maybe not. But live birds are not going to give us the luxury of letting us know when they intend to fly over us, are they? By practicing this way, the shooter's move will become more spontaneous and fluid. He needs to learn to pick his target, stand up, and move the stock of the gun smoothly toward his shoulder pocket to complete the mount.

Many times both doves and ducks are shot like this as we hide on the edge of the millet field or try to stand up in the duck blind. I promise you that a couple of lessons doing this drill with the chair will sharpen and hone muzzle control skills and gun-mounting technique.

CHAPTER 5

Learning to Shoot

Big shots are only little shots who keep shooting.

—*Christopher Morley*

Almost everyone who picks a shotgun up in the early stages is self-taught. Many years ago, at the tender age of nine, I was the same. I thought (as most do) that shooting a shotgun was an entirely natural thing, and the reason most of us think this is that everyone can hit something because of the spread of the pellets.

Many bird hunters go through their lives fooling themselves with this notion, though, mainly because they confine their shooting to the hunting season and never shoot competitively. Nobody counts their shells, so just like the gambling man, they conveniently forget their losses, but tell everyone about their hits. In fairness to these guys, in the last thirty years or so, times have dramatically changed. Due mainly to the boom in competitive shotgunning, there are now hoards of wing-shooting coaches out there. (We've always had plenty of these in the UK, but not so in the US.)

Many youngsters come to this sport through a father, uncle, or friend who loves to shoot. But even if Dad is a fabulous shot and he can stroke doves out of the sky with consummate ease and knock pheasants down in the Kansas cornfields with the best of them, that doesn't mean he is qualified to teach. Unfortunately, everyone who picks a shotgun up aspires to be a shooting coach, and I see this all the time when I am coaching at various gun clubs throughout the US.

We've all seen this, haven't we? Down at the gun club, standing on one of the practice traps on a pleasant Sunday afternoon after church, is a guy with his wife and two teenage daughters. One of the youngsters takes the stage. The young lady is a skinny fourteen-year-old, and she's noticeably a bit hesitant and apprehensive about the proceedings. Undeterred and flushed with enthusiasm, Dad thrusts the gun into her hands and shows her how to mount it.

Unfortunately, the gun is too long and too heavy. It's also a 12 gauge, and Dad is using high brass shells leftover from last year's pheasant hunt. The young lady stands with her weight correctly forward initially, but due to the weight of the gun, soon begins to wilt like a vase of abandoned flowers under the strain. Dad never notices; he's too busy explaining the finer points of the game under the admiring glances of his wife and enjoying all the attention he's getting.

Dad shows his young daughter a target and tells her in a loud voice to "put the bead on the target and pull the trigger." The young lady nods with acknowledgment and calls "Pull." Dad hits the button, and there is an orange blur as the first target is airborne. His young protégé does as she is told, pulls the trigger . . . and the target explodes in a cloud of orange dust.

All the girls are pleasantly surprised at the outcome, squealing with delight at the success. Mom and the other daughter can't wait for their turns. With the next few targets, a similar chain of events follows, and they all end up smashing some targets. Quiet confidence quickly becomes apparent. There are more squeals of delight as each target is pulverized. They are all deliriously happy, but by now, after several dozen shots each, they are starting to get sore. No problem, Dad says, it's time to wind things down for the day.

On the way home all three girls are bubbling with excitement, convinced that they are "naturals" and that dad has got to be the best shooting coach in the world.

"We've just had so much fun, darling—haven't we, girls?" says the wife, giving Dad's arm a gentle squeeze. Dad smiles smugly. Judging by the admiring glances he's getting from his better half, he knows his luck's in for the night.

The next Sunday, the same family is at the gun club again. The girls were a little sore from their first lesson, but by Wednesday, the bruises were fading. Anyway, it was worth it for the bragging rights showing off the bruises to the guys at school on Monday morning. For this next session, Dad chooses a skeet field. The eager beavers can't wait, and Mom takes up her stance on #1. The first target is missed, but Mom breaks the second. Compared with the going away targets that they all shot on the previous Sunday, the breaks on the skeet targets are patchy, but both daughters hit a few, so they move on to #2. Even fewer targets are broken here, and it becomes obvious the enthusiasm is starting to fade. In an effort to salvage the situation, Dad decides he will now show them all how to do it. Dad doesn't shoot well, and the harder he tries, the worse it gets. In desperation, he moves to #4, and the outcome there is even worse. So what went wrong? Why were they all breaking the trap-type targets last week? Was it just beginners luck?

Don't Start Learning to Shoot on a Going-Away Target

The problems stemmed from several things. First, regardless of what others may tell you, it is never advisable to start a new shooter on a trap target that is going directly away from them. In fact, the straight-away target is the worst target to start a new shooter on. There is no lead requirement on this target, so it is possible to shoot it like you would with a rifle.

Many shooting coaches start their young students on a going-away target because, quite simply, it is the easiest target to break. Think about it: A father brings his young son, Jimmy, to a shoot-

Both of these 20-gauge semiautomatics are ideal for the beginner. One is a specially modified Remington and the other is a Beretta 391 youth model.

ing coach. The coach tells young Jimmy to "put the bead on the end of the gun on the target and pull the trigger." The youngster breaks several straight-away targets on his first lesson. Dad concludes that his son is a superb natural shot and the shooting coach is the best coach in the world. But now Jimmy is looking at the end of the gun. Unless this habit is squashed immediately, it will develop into something that I call "subconscious bead fixation."

That's a mouthful, but it is a very real problem for many shooters. The worst afflicted are the rifle shooters among us. I coach many members from the Dallas Safari Club. Sometimes these members, considering a dove hunting trip to Argentina, enlist my help to teach their wives to shoot. Unfortunately, if the lady has been hunting plains game on the Serengeti with a rifle for the last 20 years, it's a safe bet, on her introduction to shotgun shooting, that she will be looking at the bead on the end of the gun. Now she has a coach with a funny accent who tells her not to, and of course, she thinks I'm an idiot! It will sometimes take me up to three hours of concentrated coaching to break the habit, and some shooters never do. For some shooters, bead fixation is like separation anxiety syndrome; they feel the need to focus on something solid.

Choose Your Gun and Ammo Wisely

The second mistake Dad made with his wife and daughters was the choice of gun. A heavy gun may not be bad up to a point because it will absorb some of the felt recoil. The tradeoff is the student's ability to swing and handle the gun efficiently. You have to make a compromise. With a gun that is just too heavy for new students, they will experience something called forward inertia, and the gun will start with a jerk as they attempt to swing it along the line of the target. Second, due to the weight of the gun, the student will be unable to keep their weight forward or nose over toes.

This youngster is keen to learn. Most aspiring young shotgunners will struggle to mount a shotgun correctly and need constant supervision in the early stages.

Third, the 12 gauge and ammunition Dad used was wrong. A whack in the face and shoulder may not be apparent with the first few shots because excitement and the flow of adrenalin deaden the pain initially. But if students are allowed to continue to feel pain, they will soon start to flinch as they trigger the shot. The pain may subside over time, but unfortunately, the flinch may remain long after, even when a more suitable gun is found. Save pain for your visits to the dentist!

Most of the time, experienced wingshooters pay a lot of attention to the things that they have control over. For example, they choose their guns carefully and then go to great lengths to have

them fitted correctly. They choose their choke selection carefully, and they choose their cartridges and shot size carefully depending on their quarry. By doing this, they believe that they will be more successful. Then they go out in the field and shoot their chosen guns without ever learning where to point them relative to the birds.

Learn to Recognize Bird/Barrel Relationships

So what is the best way to teach new shooters to recognize specific bird/barrel relationships as they trigger the shot? I always advise new shooters to shoot initially with the off-eye closed. (This is the eye that is on the opposite side of where they mount the gun.) I also prefer that they shoot with a premounted gun. This eliminates two of the variables that in the early stages of developing a library of sight pictures give many new shooters a problem. A premounted gun ensures that the butt is in the correct place before calling for the target. The closed eye means that the eye above the barrel is the one that is being relied on for the correct bird/barrel relationship. As soon as a correct sight picture is recognized, the shooter can then attempt to reapply it with both eyes open. Just like a visit to the optometrist I ask if the sight picture is better or worse. If, with two eyes, the student cannot repeat the break, I suspect a weak dominance problem. This is very common with young shooters whose central nervous systems are not fully developed.

The three main shooting methods for applying forward allowance are swing-through, pull-away, and sustained lead. Many attempts have been made to rationalize ways to apply lead, and over many decades, countless pages have been written on the subject, but these are the main contenders. For each of these, you need to see a target/barrel relationship as you take the shot.

Swing-Through

If the bird is moving when you pull the trigger, the muzzles need to be pointing at a spot somewhere in front of the bird. Most self-taught bird hunters and those who are taught by someone else shoot swing-through because it is simple. You mount the gun and swing through the line of the bird, triggering the shot as you do this.

Swing-through works because anyone using any shotgun can swing the gun more or less onto the line of the target without knowing anything about lead, gun fit, gun mount, or master eye and manage to hit something. Some call swing-through, which originated in the UK, the instinc-

tive method. Probably the man who came closest to convincing everyone that there was one foolproof method of applying lead, which would triumph over all the others, was Robert Churchill.

His famous English or instinctive shooting method was for many years the preferred one (sometimes the only one) that was taught at the majority of the shooting schools in England. In the US, the method is taught at the Orvis Shooting School. Success with this method depends entirely on basic hand-eye coordination and a smooth follow-through. The speed of the gun builds in the necessary lead. According to Churchill, his method was so superior to every other that there was never the slightest hint of lead or forward allowance necessary. Does it work? Sometimes.

Let's take a look at shooting birds with this method. For the purpose of our calculations, let's assume that the bird is flying at approximately 50 mph at approximately 90 degrees to the shooting position and approximately 20 yards away. Let's also assume that the shot load is traveling at 1,200 fps, which is 800 mph. This means that for every yard the bird flies, the cloud of pellets will travel 16 yards, or an approximate ratio of 16:1.

If the gun, as it swings through from behind the target, is traveling at about two or three times the speed of the target, this reduces the apparent lead (the amount of lead the shooter thinks he needs to see) and he believes he is shooting more or less directly at the bird. As the shooter sees his gun pointing directly at the bird, he gives his brain the signal to fire. During the slight delay of the shooter's reaction time and the shot column reaching the target, the bird will travel about 4 feet or so. But the gun is moving a lot faster than the bird. So as the shot charge exits the barrel, the gun is pointing approximately 3 or 4 feet in front of the bird, and a direct hit is the result when the pellets eventually arrive there. This is why some wingshooters tell you they never see lead.

Most wingshooters shoot behind birds. How often have you missed a long shot at a dove or duck with your first shot, only to connect with it on your second? Why does that happen? It's merely the way that a predatory animal reacts to prey that is escaping. Think of a kitten playing with a ball of wool. If the kitten misses with its first pounce, the next one is often quicker, and it connects.

We do the same with shotgunning. If we miss a rapidly accelerating dove, we panic, and without thinking, our spontaneous reaction to the escaping bird is an instinctive increase in our gun speed. This is why the Churchill method is successful sometimes. For bird hunting, that's OK. Sometimes it works, and we put another bird in the bag. But if you teach someone to shoot by using a swing-through method, although by the law of averages he will manage to hit some birds some of the time, it is doubtful if he will learn anything from the experience and will continue to hit most of his birds by pure luck.

With swing-through shooting, you have two other variables that you can't control as you take the shot: swing speed and your reaction time. If either of these varies, even slightly, hit consistency will be out the window. That's the main reason that the method is seldom used for competitive shotgunning. A shooter's reaction time is simply the time it takes for his brain to respond to the signal to trigger the shot plus the time it takes for the firing pin to hit the primer. Erratic gun speeds also cause problems with swing-through. With a fast swing, you need to see less apparent lead; with a slow swing, you need to see more. With a gun speed of about two or three times the target speed, the apparent lead would be zero. This is the essence of the Churchill shooting method for bird hunting.

Another problem is that the increase in gun speed will produce a huge amount of momentum and forward inertia in the gun, which will have the tendency to move the gun in a straight line. In other words, once you apply excessive gun speed, any deviation the bird makes from a reasonably straight flight trajectory will be difficult to develop accurately. The result is that you are committed, due to this momentum, to triggering the shot when your gun is on the line that the bird isn't on!

Many coaches teach the method because anyone can hit something by using it, which makes the shooting coach look good. But it doesn't really teach us anything. All it means is some of the birds are hit some of the time, and some of the time you actually know why. But for consistency, it has its shortfalls. This is why only a very small minority of shooters use it in a competitive environment.

Pull-Away

In pull-away, like swing-through, calculating the window of opportunity is difficult because as you trigger the shot, you accelerate the gun away from the bird. If you insert the muzzle on the front edge of the bird and pull away, assuming your gun is moving just slightly faster than the target, the muzzle will still need to be pointing at a spot about 4 feet in front of the bird as you pull the trigger. You still need a visual clue to decide to pull the trigger. How do you decide just how far (and how fast) to pull away on each bird?

Some successful bird hunters have told me that they can insert the gun on the bird and then pull away on the same line until they trigger the shot. By doing this, they can keep the bird in focus better, rather than losing it momentarily (as it vanishes behind the gun) as it does with a swing-through shot. But once again, if the bird makes even a slight deviation from its flight line (and most birds have the annoying habit of doing just that), as with the swing-through method, the gun may make an errant move on the wrong line as the shot is triggered.

This shows that any shooting method that relies on irregular gun speed and shooter reaction time to provide the necessary forward allowance on a bird, instead of a visual cue, will offer a narrow window of opportunity and doubtful consistency.

Sustained Lead

Let's look at the sustained lead method—in my opinion, a vastly superior method to any other for teaching someone to shoot. This method is the only method that gives a shotgunner a clear indication of how much visual lead is required on each target. A properly executed sustained-lead shot synchronizes the gun and target speeds, leaving no residual gun movement as you trigger the shot—a real boost to shot-to-shot consistency. This in turn makes shooter reaction time inconsequential, so the window of opportunity is more or less infinite, providing the shooter has in his mind a visual indication of when he should pull the trigger based on the angle, speed, and range of the bird.

The unit lead method in chapter 8 teaches you how to do this. The beauty of sustained lead is that the shooter can respond to any directional change the bird makes before—not as—he triggers each shot. His muzzles are always in front of the bird, and he always maintains visual contact with it. He can respond to exactly what the bird is doing as it does it and yet still remain on the same line. I feel that seeing what the bird is doing as you trigger the shot is a huge advantage.

I am not trying to debunk the Churchill method or any other method; I'm just presenting the facts from having observed and coached many thousands of shotgunners. The swing-through shooters will hit birds some of the time, but usually birds at modest range. They hit these birds purely because the gun is moving faster than the bird. They are not relying on a visual indication of how much lead they need to see. When swing-through shooters are presented with birds at extended ranges—ducks, pheasant, doves, and so on—they swing the gun even more rapidly to give more forward allowance, but the problem is it's impossible to move the gun fast enough to give the required lead and remain in control of the gun. Birds don't fly in straight lines. Erratic gun

movement will mean that the gun will not trace the same flight line as the bird. A miss is inevitable.

To illustrate this point better, a mile down the road from where I lived in Scotland was Westerhall Estate, and some of the best driven pheasants in the world, and I would sometimes load for the visiting guns. Many of them, very familiar with the instinctive method that was at one time the only method taught at the shooting schools of the south of England, would find the birds impossible to hit until I explained that they should see a lot more daylight as they pulled the trigger, especially on the crossing birds. Just exactly how much daylight? Well, a quick calculation revealed that if the pheasant was flying at 40 mph and was 40 yards away, the lead requirement was at least 9 or 10 feet. Extend the range to the maximum, about 50 to 55 yards, and they needed at least 14 or 15 feet.

Many of the visiting guns, who had been taught the instinctive method, would find their performance hopelessly inadequate at these extended ranges, and they would resort to a quick flick of the gun at the end of their swing in a desperate attempt to put the gun farther in front of the bird. Unfortunately this flick would often pull the gun off-line, and they would miss either to the left or right of the bird. In the US I have witnessed the same thing many times when dove hunters are presented with a long shot. Many dove hunters let the bird approach, realize that it needs a huge amount of lead, but because they have never learned how much, let the bird fly past them. They then swing through the bird as it passes at an alarming speed, in a desperate attempt to connect. This approach has never made much sense to me, and in my opinion, it is never very successful.

Swing-through and pull-away *can* be used with success in many bird hunting situations. For example, in many situations in the field, the bird will manifest itself when the muzzles are already behind it, so you'll have to use swing-through. But it must be controlled swing-through or controlled pull-away without relying on aggressive gun movement, after you have learned how far in front of the bird you need to be. Look for a visual clue, with the gun moving in harmony with the bird, by first learning to shoot with the sustained lead method. Once these sight pictures are locked and loaded into your hard drive, it is a simple matter of adjusting your timing and gun speed to accommodate a swing-through or pull-away technique, as necessary.

To wingshoot successfully, consider four variables as you pull the trigger.

1. Your ability to move the gun exactly on the same line as the bird.
2. Your ability to approximately judge range of the bird.
3. Your ability to approximately judge the angle of the bird.
4. Your ability to approximately judge the speed of the bird.

Of these four variables, the line and angle have the biggest impact on success. You become successful when you hunt birds by building up, over a period of time, a mental repertoire of sight pictures that you know to be correct. The unit lead method will help with this, and once you establish this repertoire of sight pictures, you will shoot more intuitively. Instead of poking and hoping, you will rely on a much more reliable technique for hunting forays and eventually transform those frustrating whiffs into confident hits.

CHAPTER 6

Lead 'Em, Laddie!

When I was but a little boy and scarce could lift the gun,
I oft would leave each childish toy, and to the fields would run.
With Pistol for my fowling-piece, I thought myself a man,
And thus improving by degrees, a Sportsman's life began.

—*William Henry Scott*

It was early springtime on Lord Egerton's estate, and the cock pheasants, resplendent in their breeding plumage, were strutting their stuff to impress the dowdy hens. The previous year's pheasant and partridge shoots had gone well. Now the keepers, with their wallets bursting at the seams with the tips from the well-heeled clients, were busy laying the foundation for the new season. It was a critical time for them. Vermin needed to be culled wherever possible to reduce their numbers and keep predation to a minimum.

Me, Andy, and the dogs were walking in a thick hedgerow, Andy on one side, me on the other, hoping for a shot at a magpie, crow, or perhaps even a stoat or weasel. These diminutive, bloodthirsty members of the Muscidae family paired up in the spring. They would wreak havoc in the pheasant coverts, and their presence was not tolerated by the keepers.

Andy had tunnel traps set in several locations along the hedgerow. As we walked the hedgerow to check the traps, a carrion crow, with plumage as black as his heart, slipped silently from his cover in a holly tree and crossed in front of us about 30 yards away. Carrion crows have a nasty reputation, and no keeper worth his salt can afford to have one on his patch. They will kill all young fledglings in any nest they find and take all the young game bird chicks they can eat. But the real problem is their ability to seek out and destroy the nests of the ground-nesting pheasants and partridge. Once they find a nest, a pair of crows will systematically return until every egg is destroyed.

"Shoot the crow, lad!" Andy bellowed. I was momentarily mesmerized, but I did as I was told; my gun came up, and I gave the crow both barrels. It was blind panic. In the heat of the moment, in the brief time lapse between seeing the crow and the gun coming up, I had absolutely no idea where my gun was pointing relative to the target. It was a true poke-and-hope shot, and I would probably been better using a peashooter. I never touched a feather and the crow never flinched, but Andy saved the day. His gun came up unerringly into his shoulder, crashed once, and the crow, perhaps 50 yards away by now, fell as dead as a mack.

It was a good shot; in fact I would go so far as to say an exceptional shot, and Andy knew it. He never minced his words, and he turned to me with triumphant grin on his face.

"You gotta lead 'em, boy! No use shootin' at 'em, you gotta lead 'em," he said with a knowing wink. Of course, then I remembered. Andy had always drummed it into me.

"Shoot where the bird's going, laddie, not where he's been!" he would say. But in those highly charged few seconds, Andy's teachings had, unfortunately, gone in one ear and out the other.

Later in the day, we stopped for a bite to eat. I always asked questions, probably too many, but I was curious to know how Andy had dispatched the carrion crow with apparent ease when I wasn't even close.

"So how much do you lead 'em by, Andy?" I asked. We were sitting in one of our favorite places, a giant, fallen oak tree on the edge of a hazel thicket.

Andy gulped the last mouthful of tea from his flask cup and then, as he stood up, splashed the remaining dregs onto the ground. He ambled unhurriedly to a nearby hazel bush, snapped a long stick off and expertly stripped the leaves from it by running it through his gnarled hand. In the sandy soil underneath the mighty oak, Andy scratched a crude diagram with the hazel stick. Andy's sketching in the dirt depicted a bird travelling at approximately 90 degrees to his shooting position.

"This bird, lad," Andy said thoughtfully, tapping the sketch on the ground with his stick, "needs a big lead, a goose wing, maybe four fingers." Andy held his gnarled fist up next to the muzzles of his old side-by-side AYA to indicate how much he was meaning.

Then he scratched another diagram showing an approximate 45-degree angle. "This bird," he continued, "needs less, a pheasant's wing, perhaps a two-finger lead," he said, as he held two fingers next to his gun.

And the birds coming in or going out at a narrow angle to our shooting position? Andy said these were all partridge-wing leads, perhaps a one-finger lead, or small amount of forward allowance.

At first, I was puzzled. What did he mean by a goose-wing lead that was four fingers at the muzzle? But eventually the light came on for me. What Andy was indicating was that we see lead in one of two places, either out there at the target—in other words on the full 90-degree crossing shot, the goose wing—or at the muzzle of the gun, which correlated roughly into a four-finger lead.

Andy's crude yet effective description worked, and I found myself applying fingers of lead as each situation arose. In a short space of time, this was easy for me to do. I found myself thinking as a crow or similar bird broke cover and flew at an angle of approximately 90 degrees to me, "Aha, he needs a big, four-finger lead, like this" as I triggered the shot. Or for a duck, extricating himself from the bulrush (cattail) margins of a reed bed almost directly in front, much less lead was required because of the reduced angle. This narrow-angle shot was a one-finger lead.

In a very short time, my brain became programmed, but now I was shooting intuitively not instinctively. There is a difference. I also began to shoot where the bird was going, in other words, into the anticipated flight path of the bird. By applying Andy's angular methodology, I now knew more precisely where to place my shot charge and I bagged more birds. Andy was a big, rough-around-the-edges sort of guy, but I think of him still. In his inimitable way he passed on to me the benefit of his years of experience as a keeper. Little did I know that what I learned all those years ago would later be useful as a learning tool for my bird hunting clients.

Seeing Lead

Lead, forward allowance, call it what you will. If the target is moving, you can't shoot at it. Over the years, I have had conversations with many bird hunters about lead, and they have revealed some interesting things. Many of them swear that they never see lead of any sort as they shoot. For a shooting coach, this is frustrating, because most of the time these guys will be missing their birds behind.

Recently, I had a conversation with one of these guys who was a keen dove hunter. We were at the Elmfork facility in Dallas. The targets were coming over him at thirty yards plus from the hundred foot tower. He was missing every target behind, and I asked him, as he triggered each shot, how much lead he saw.

"Lead? Oh, I never see lead!" he replied indignantly, "I just swing the gun and pull the trigger. I manage to hit some of them."

I very nearly replied that, because he was shooting behind them all, he would need to double his lead. But then I thought better of it. It isn't easy to tell someone to double his lead if he never saw any in the first place, is it?

Calculating Lead

Some shooting coaches will tell you, in bird hunting situations, that it is hopeless to try to calculate lead. Later, when they are sitting in the duck blind, they go into lengthy details about why, when a flock of greenheads skim across the decoys at a distance, you need to "lead 'em by a truck length." Well, maybe I'm mistaken, but isn't that a form of calculation?

Most bird hunters seldom, if ever, consider the variables of speed, distance, or trajectory. They handle their chosen piece once a year (usually the day before dove season) and venture into the field with the hope that they manage to hit something with it. For many of them, these annual forays are just coincidental encounters, nothing more. There is no intentional objective to ensure the correct convergence of bird and shot column. In other words, connecting with the occasional bird is nothing more than a lucky accident! If that isn't the case, then how come the guys that do consider the variables before they shoot—in other words, the competitive skeet and sporting clay guys—develop into such damn fine bird shots in the field?

With its wide pattern, the shotgun is a forgiving weapon, and anybody can hit something with one. These days, you need only go to a sporting clay charity fundraiser or charity corporate event to see this. Participants who have never before picked up a shotgun in their lives manage to hit something. That is one of the main reasons events of this sort are growing in popularity. But that doesn't mean that these participants understand what they are doing.

Some shooting coaches will tell you that it is impossible to calculate and then implement specific lead pictures (especially in bird hunting situations) because the variables are constantly changing. I do not agree. The human brain is an amazing thing; it is perfectly capable of processing visual information in a nanosecond. But the brain is also like a computer; you must first load the information onto your hard drive order to download it when you need it. We all become accomplished shots (over a period of time) by building up a personal, mental repertoire of sight pictures that we know to be correct.

I use a simple visual aid to demonstrate to my students how much lead they need to see on a target, and it helps enormously. When I first moved here from the UK, one of my early students was so impressed that he said I should patent the device. I replied that it was a black button from Walmart that was fixed onto the end of a telescopic car aerial from Radio Shack. The client missed the point. The device only works because I know the bird/barrel relationship and can demonstrate this by holding the pointer next to the gun.

Once your hard drive has stored this information, you recognize which sight picture is the correct one to apply to each specific situation and another bird is in the bag. When faced with multiple birds, in quail hunting for example, one of the main reasons bird hunters flock-shoot is because they don't know how much lead they need. They have never taken the time to build up a repertoire of sight pictures. Pray and spray. Poke and hope. Poke and pray. It's all the same, I'm afraid.

After a few lessons, many of my clients think nothing of shooting crossing doves at ranges of 40 yards plus. Before the lessons, this type of shot

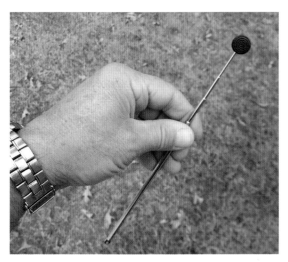

This is the small "target on a stick" telescopic pointer that I use to illustrate to my clients how much lead they need at the muzzle with a given target.

would be impossible for them. This range is the limit of a shotgun, but one pellet in a dove's head at 40 yards and, make no mistake, he's in the bag. Five pellets in his butt and he isn't. We miss shots like this because of plain ol' pilot error. We just don't know where to put the shot pattern relative to the target . . . but we can learn.

Success with a Shotgun

Learning to shoot a shotgun successfully takes time. Learning any new hand-eye coordination skill takes time, whether it's golf, tennis, or baseball. But for some reason, some shooters think shotgun skills are different somehow. You know some guys who hope to become accomplished shots without putting the time in, but I have never seen an expert shot get there by God's grace and natural ability alone. These guys go out on hunting trips without really understanding what they're doing and hope that on this particular day God will smile down on them and they will manage to hit something. Some days they do, but most days they don't. At the end of the day, they are uncomfortable, disillusioned, and have an empty game bag. This failure in the field soon develops into frustration and desperation. In an effort to justify the expense of the cost of the pheasant, duck, dove, or quail lease; the expensive guns; the Kawasaki mule; and the dogs, they make excuses. "There's not many doves about this year near San Antonio," they say. "It's not cold enough for the ducks in Arkansas" or "The fire ants have destroyed the quail population in West Texas." And you know what? I suspect that most of these guys, on the long drive home as they kick the blank days on the hunting lease around in their heads, are never really comfortable with their performance because they never really understand why they are missing. Usually these are the guys that develop some sort of psychosis when it comes to taking instruction.

Our ability to become a successful shot, according to most people, is based on our ability to concentrate. Concentrate on what? On the end of the gun? Our fingernails? The sky? When I first arrived in the US in 1997, I began writing articles for some of the shooting magazines. Some of the information I read in these magazines was mystifying to me. At that time, the popular opinion among all the shooting coaches, no exceptions, was that the one thing we must focus on as we trigger the shot is the target, be it bird or clay.

All the coaches agreed, however, that our success with a shotgun also depended on a gun that was a perfect fit and that we must develop the ability to mount it correctly. Then, and only then, will the gun shoot where we look. I agree. But their obsession with concentrating and visually focusing on the target as you trigger the shot had me more than slightly baffled. Some coaches even take this a step further and tell you (when talking about live birds) to focus on the beak and (when talking about clay targets) to focus so intently on the target that you can see the rings on the top.

Now, I think I have pretty good eyesight. More important, I know many master class shooters and terrific bird hunters who have amazing eyesight. But I don't know anyone who can truthfully say he can see the rings clearly on a rapidly spinning clay target at range of more than ten yards or so. At twenty yards and greater, I just don't believe you can see any rings at all.

Shooting coaches insist that you must have a gun that fits and when you do the gun will shoot where you look. So if the gun does shoot where you look, out in the field, on the long shot at the dove, duck, or pheasant—where the lead requirement at the target may be several feet or more—and if we are still looking at the target as we trigger the shot, where does the lead come from?

Back to the earlier point about concentration. Many years ago, when I was employed at the Dallas Gun Club, in Lewisville, Texas, I held a clinic with two very successful shooting coaches who were very well established in the US. Between us, we had about thirty students, and we split them into three groups. On the sporting clay course, one of the stations was a pair of full crossing shots coming off the high tower at a distance of perhaps 50 yards or so. All the shooters were struggling on these full crossing targets. As one of the guys in my group missed target after target, I asked him what he was concentrating on as he triggered the shot. The shooter looked both perplexed and slightly indignant and then replied, "I'm looking at the target, of course!"

Of course, I knew he was, and I also knew that was exactly why he was missing them. Every shot he triggered was going behind the target. So I continued, "This time, I would like you to focus intently on the target and at the split second you trigger the shot, I would like you to look in front of it a distance of what you would consider to be 10 to 12 feet and instantly trigger the shot."

The client looked puzzled but with a shrug of his shoulders did as I asked. Lo and behold, the targets began breaking with almost monotonous consistency. He was ecstatic and a triumphant cheer went up from his group.

"What did he tell you?" I heard one guy ask. As the shooter explained to his group that I had instructed him to shoot at a spot in front of the target, they were dumbfounded. But it worked.

So why was the guy missing? There was no doubt in my mind that he was missing because of overconcentrating on the target. The vast majority of shooters have the mantra "focus intently on the target" drummed into them. In fact, most shooting coaches will tell you that if your gun fits, it will shoot where you look. These same coaches will then also tell you that as you trigger the shot, you should always focus 100 percent on the bird. But if our well-fitted and perfectly mounted shotguns point where we are looking, concentrating on the bird as we trigger the shot, instead of the appropriate point ahead of it, must give rise to missing.

We may be able to deal with several things at the same time, but we can only concentrate on one. This guy, as he triggered the shot, was still looking at the target. The result on this full crossing shot (that may have required 12 feet or more lead at the target) was that by the time the shot column reached the target, his pattern was going exactly where he intended it to go, approximately 12 feet behind the target!

Now, this sort logic is not what many shooting coaches will tell you, and many people reading this will reject this advice out of hand. But to those people, I say this. Sometimes, we accept the opinion of others without question, without attempting to form our own opinion. In another attempt to brass my case I offer further advice and examples from two of the best shots in the world.

The first example is from an article that appeared in *Clay Shooting USA* magazine in December 2005. The article was about how to hit long crossers by Richard Faulds, who was at that time the current World and European FITASC Champion. He wrote:

> If your gun fit and mount are correct, your eyes should do all the work. On a short range target it is usually sufficient to lock your eyes onto the leading edge of the clay to hit it. As distance increases a conscious gap needs to be established. Lock onto the clay briefly to give your brain the vital data on line and speed and then look out ahead of it to where you want to place your shot and fire. Your gun will follow your eyes naturally. Want more lead? Look further ahead. Do it positively, do not look back to check.

Another example is from an article that appeared in the December 1998 issue of *Sporting Clays* magazine. This excellent article, "Stellar Star of the Game," was written by Nick Sisley about Jon Kruger, who was at that time the US champion:

> You've heard the axiom over and over "Look at the target, look at the target." Surprisingly, this isn't what Kruger does. Instead, he tries to focus on a spot somewhere out ahead of the target. Why? Because that's where his shot-string has to go. Once he, or any of us, pull the trigger, there is a time-lapse between then and the time it takes the shot charge to get to the bird. This is why lead is essential.

So there it is. Expert advice from both sides of the Atlantic. By their own admission, these guys do *not* look at the target as they trigger the shot; they look in front of it.

You may be thinking, "That's competitive shotgunning. I'm a bird hunter, so this doesn't apply to me." But it does. The idea that competitive skeet and sporting clays ruins bird hunting skills is another myth. To be successful at the sport of clay target shooting depends on your ability to intercept a target with a cloud of pellets. To be a successful bird hunter depends on your ability to intercept a target with a cloud of pellets. They are no different. The bird travelling at approximately 50 mph needs exactly the same lead as the clay target going the same speed. But the hard part is deciding just how far in front of the target you must look before you pull the trigger. Chapter 8, the unit lead method, will show you how to do this.

CHAPTER 7

Timing and Shooting to a Rhythm

See the bird and watch him come,

But never ever mount the gun,

Too quickly, it's not straight he flies,

He bobs and weaves before your eyes.

Move the muzzles, his path to plot,

But only mount to take the shot.

—*Peter F. Blakeley*

Watch a really good quail, dove, pheasant, or duck hunter as he harvests his birds. A stylish shot seems to move unhurriedly, blending his barrels with unerring accuracy onto the line of each bird, his muzzles slicing the air with the grace and precision of the sword wielded by the samurai warrior. The guy who, on the dove hunt, as the other hunters are flailing wildly with the gyrations of a Turkish belly dancer, strokes the birds from the sky with a composed elegance. Or the quail hunter who seems to have the uncanny knack of picking the right spot, the bird, and the right time—and seldom misses. Out in the field or at the gun club, we all talk about these guys in hushed whispers.

When I lived in Scotland, I had the pleasure of observing many fine shots, especially on the driven pheasant and grouse shoots. The majority of these experienced guys possessed an unhurried elegance as they triggered their shots. One such guy who I observed on many occasions was Patrick Hope-Johnstone, the Earl of Annandale. Another was the late Peter Buckley of Westerhall Estate. On the competitive front, some of the top sporting clay shots—George Digweed, Scott Robertson, and Jon Kruger—are the same, as are some of the world's top skeet shooters.

Robert Paxton, Todd Bender, and Wayne Mayes spring to mind. All these guys have one thing in common: absolutely impeccable timing and unhurried elegance. They appear to move in slow motion. Simply put, they all make it look easy. Without timing or rhythm in the shot, we shoot hurriedly, we shoot erratically, and most important of all, we generally shoot badly.

I know lots of shooting coaches, but I don't know any who suggest shooting to a rhythm in bird hunting situations. In the introduction for this book I said that it would be an educational book, with a genuine intent to try to help put a few more birds in your bag. I believe that most of us lack this personal timing, but we can learn to improve this and increase our average.

Put it this way: When hunting flushing birds over dogs, many of us would agree that our misses are caused by the gun going off prematurely due to a reflex as we are startled by the sudden appearance of the bird. Honestly, isn't that what happens? Even good, solid competitive skeet and sporting clay shots can crash and burn when it comes to shooting live birds out in the field. Most of the time, this is due mainly to the sudden unannounced appearance of the bird, which causes erratic gun mounting, hurried muzzle movement, and premature trigger pulling before the correct bird/barrel relationship is seen. There is a way to greatly reduce the tendency to do this, but it takes practice.

Years ago, I read a book written by a prominent tennis coach, whose name, if I remember correctly, was Le Couilliard. He found that during his coaching sessions, many of his young students experienced difficulty in returning the ball over the net with any consistency. He also found that if he got them to return the ball by reciting a rally progression rhythm, their consistency improved dramatically. The rhythm was Ball (as their eyes locked onto the ball), Bounce (as the ball bounced before the net), and Hit (as the racquet connected with the ball to return it over the net).

In an earlier chapter, I suggested that when we quail hunt we should learn to shoot to a rhythm. There is nothing new in this; the Brits have been doing something similar for years. For example, the driven pheasant rhythm is Butt, Belly, Beak, Bang. But there are others, including one or two that I have modified during my coaching years, and they work extremely well.

As ridiculous as it may seem, many quail/flushing bird hunters shoot a mite too fast. Our brains are easily capable of deciphering the variables of the bird with lightning speed and always operate far quicker than our bodies are capable of responding to. Simply put, the old saying about the hand being quicker than the eye is very true. Our bodies will respond to visual input if we let them.

Most quail hunters become hopelessly overwhelmed because the initial adrenalin rush of the sudden appearance of the covey overpowers their senses. Then, rather than picking their bird, in desperation, they flock-shoot. This also occurs not just with quail but most shots over pointing and flushing dogs. Always remember, there isn't a bird out there that can fly faster than the pellets of your shot-string. If you can find a way to minimize gun movement and maximize visual acuity of the target, you will put more birds in the bag.

When any of us use a shotgun, what we are doing is converting visual information into physical movement to intuitively put the gun in the right place as we trigger the shot. If we don't allow our brains time to compute this visual information (and most of us don't), the gun doesn't move into the correct position to intercept the target and we miss. It's back to poke-and-hope or poke-and-pray shotgunning. Shooting rhythmically helps us to overcome this problem and allows the visual input to register correctly. The difference between a poke-and-hope shot and an intuitive judgment shot may be only a millisecond, just enough time for our brain to compute the variables and visual input and accurately position the gun.

One of the other main reasons we miss birds is that we don't get into the gun correctly as we trigger the shot. When the birds appear suddenly and we are desperate to get a shot off, we shoot while the gun is still out of our shoulders and our heads are off the comb. We get bruised arms, bruised faces, and our eyes, the back sight of the shotgun, are nowhere near where they should be. We'll have no idea where the gun is pointing relative to the bird as we trigger the shot. Shooting to a rhythm will help to solve this problem also.

I like to call the type of birds we hunt flushers and flashers. This categorization always raises a smile to my clients' faces, but when they try the rhythms I suggest for each for themselves in the field, they are pleasantly surprised to find that they do indeed work. A bird classed as a flusher is any bird that is put up at reasonably close quarters as it emerges from cover, either over pointing dogs or flushing dogs.

Narrow-Angle Targets

Most birds that are hunted over pointing or flushing dogs are narrow-angle targets. Most quail species, walked-up Scottish red grouse, Kansas cornfield pheasant, Hungarian partridge, ruffed grouse, and woodcock fall into this category. You must shoot these birds reasonably quickly to a three-beat rhythm because they will be most vulnerable to your gun then. Most of the time three seconds is all you get before they have either vanished behind

If you can get permission to do this, walking up on the trap machine at your local gun club is excellent practice for stepping to the bird to make sure your weight is over your leading leg as you trigger the shot.

cover or accelerated directly away from you quickly, thus covering their most vital organ, their head.

So what is the best way to hone your skills for a flusher hunt? Obviously one-on-one coaching is best, but I will try to describe exactly how I do this during a training lesson. If possible, a clay target launcher with someone else pulling the targets is ideal. Today, individual clay target machines can be bought for a modest price. If this isn't an option, the ATA machine at your local shooting facility will do.

Stand behind the machine for your first few shots, with the targets going directly away from you. At this stage, you will call for the target to be released. Watch the target, and you will see that as it accelerates away from you, it is also rising. If it is rising, then you must shoot slightly above it. Shoot the targets at first with a premounted gun to eliminate the possibility of missing the mount. As you see the target, raise the gun smoothly onto the line—just cover it up and trigger the shot immediately. Do this a few times until you know what sight picture you need to see to break the target.

Then stand on the left of the machine and do the same again. Now the target will be going slightly right to left, so you will need to give it a small amount of lead. Once again, shoot the target a few times so you understand the sight picture required to break it. Then stand on the right side of the machine, and do the same thing again. These sight pictures will register subconsciously, so you will have a few sight pictures to apply to hunting situations.

Next, do the same thing again, but this time, the person pulling the targets should not announce them and you should not call "Pull!" For the first targets, you can stand in one position with the gun elevated approximately 30 to 40 degrees to the horizontal. The position of the gun is paramount in developing economy of movement.

This time, the gun should be just out of your shoulder, as if you are standing behind dogs on a point. This time, shoot the targets to a rhythm. The rhythm for all flushing birds is the three-beat rhythm, *bird, beak, bang!* (See next page.)

Practice this drill until you become competent and can break most of the targets. Next, stand about 20 feet behind the machine. Start walking forward slowly as though you are walking up on pointing dogs. Targets should be released randomly as before. Don't forget that a clay target launcher will be sending a target out at approximately 50 mph, which is a lot faster than a flushed bird that has just become airborne. And don't forget that clay targets will be travelling on a more or less straight trajectory, unlike live birds.

This drill is great practice for stepping to the bird and making sure your weight is over the leading leg as you trigger each shot. If possible, use a machine throwing variable targets rather than a static machine. The ultimate quail hunting simulator is several machines that oscillate from side to side to give a very lifelike covey rise. The birds are randomly released by computer, and I have installed many of these at private ranches throughout the US.

Shooting to a rhythm like this does seem like a strange thing to do, but it works, I promise you. Most of my clients call me with glowing reports of improvement with their flushing bird hunting skills after they have mastered this technique.

Wide Incoming Targets

Now about those flashers. Most of the birds I categorize as flashers are speeding birds, either crossing or passing shots, wide incoming angles, or driven incoming shots. Birds that fall into this category are doves, driven pheasants, grouse and partridge, and ducks coming into decoys. They are birds that you can see approaching for a long time. With this type of shot, there is always more time than you think.

Sometimes when I suggest shooting to a rhythm to some of my students at a dove clinic,

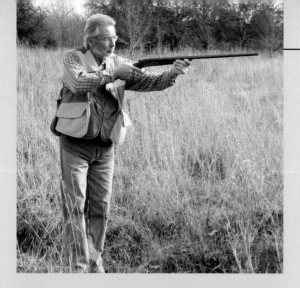

Bird, Beak, Bang!

1. BIRD. Here the gun is just out of my shoulder and I am walking forward toward the dog and a possible flush. I would do the same thing if I was practicing on clay targets.

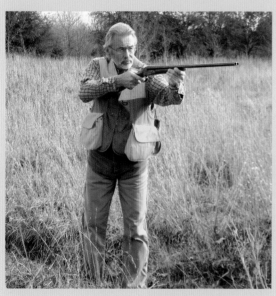

2. BEAK. A target is released, or in actual hunting situations the bird flushes and flies from left to right. I take a step in the direction the target/bird is moving, and at the same time the gun is moving toward my shoulder. By taking this step, my shoulders will remain level. I try to focus on the leading edge of the target or the beak of one of the birds and lock onto it in hard focus.

3. BANG. In this picture the gun is firmly seated in my shoulder and my leading leg is pointing toward the bird/target as I trigger the shot.

This rooster pheasant flushes in front of the hunter and flies from left to right in front of him. As the pheasant does this, the hunter's feet are almost side by side.

In this second picture, taken a millisecond later, the hunter correctly takes another step in the direction the rooster is travelling; in other words, he steps to the bird. His shoulders remain level, his weight is correctly over his leading leg, and he moves smoothly onto the bird to develop his line.

I'm sure they think I'm crazy. One of these clients, despite taking lessons from several shooting coaches in the past, had never heard of anything like it before. This particular guy had very little natural rhythm, but he was passionate about his dove and driven pheasant hunting. During a lesson on the one-hundred-foot-plus high tower at the Elmfork facility, I pulled a few targets for him. We were probably at least fifty to sixty yards from the base of the tower, so the targets seemed to take forever to reach our shooting position. As soon as the target was spotted in the distance, this client would immediately jam his gun into his shoulder as fast as possible. Then he would track the target all the way in until it came into range, where he would trigger the shot. Needless to say, he didn't hit many of them. There is little point in mounting the gun firmly into your shoulder pocket until you intend to use it.

I've witnessed this scenario many times on driven pheasant shoots in Scotland. Inexperienced shots, seeing the birds approach over the tops of trees will often do the same thing. Once again, as in the fast flushing birds of the covey rise of the quail hunt, I'm sure the adrenalin rush is to blame; experienced shots don't do this.

It's wrong for several reasons. First and foremost, the longer the gun is in your shoulder, the more you are aware of it. Second, with the gun in this premounted position, any subtle nuance that the bird makes with its line of flight will be difficult to decipher, because the gun is central to your line of vision, and you will attempt to see the target through the mounted gun. Third, tracking the bird all the way in often leads to measuring, and you may be tempted to shift visual focus from the bird to the end of the gun. The final and most important reason is that birds don't fly in straight lines. If you put the gun in your shoulder early and then attempt to move it, you'll have trouble developing the line. Birds that you can see for longer than a few seconds need a

different, four-beat rhythm. The rhyme to use with this four-beat rhythm is *polly put the kettle on* or my simplified version *that bird is going there.* This is how it works.

A skeet field is ideal for this practice. With the gun in a low gun position, well out of your shoulder, call for a target. Your call of "Pull" is the first beat of the rhythm, or the first word of the rhyme *(Polly)*. Start your gun mount, and as you do, recite the words to yourself. Move the gun slowly at first, but become progressively slightly faster, eventually completing the mount as you get to the fourth beat of the rhythm *(on* in the rhyme). You should trigger the shot as soon as the gun locks into your face and shoulder on the fourth beat. As you trigger the shot, the only thing you should be looking at is a moving spot that you perceive to be in front of the target. In other words, you are trying to imagine where the target/bird will be by the time your shot pattern reaches it. You look in front for the smallest fraction of time.

This may be different advice from what you have heard before. You may have heard that you should stay focused on the target/bird even as you trigger the shot. But the looking in front of the target method works because if your gun fits, it will shoot where you look. If you are still looking at the target as you trigger the shot, you will hit exactly what you are pointing the gun at, the space where the target was when you pulled the trigger. If the target is about twenty yards away and crossing at approximately 90 degrees to your shooting position, your shot will reach a spot that's about four feet behind it. Repositioning your eyes to a place in front of the target is the way all the top guys shoot, no exceptions.

Do this exercise several times, and then change positions on the skeet field and do the same thing again. Call for each target as before. Now you will have a completely different angle and range to consider, but if you have absorbed all the information in the unit lead section, your brain should interpret these new variables by the time the gun comes into your shoulder. Because you can see the target for a considerable time, the four-beat rhythm allows your brain the time it needs to decipher the variables of the new angle and range. Once again, trigger the shot as soon as the gun comes snugly into your shoulder pocket. Move around the skeet field to different positions until you become more confident.

The next stage is a bit more complicated, but it will be as near as you can get to actual bird hunting situations in the field. Your puller should begin releasing the targets without warning. The first time I try this with my clients, the effect is quite comical.

"Hold on, Pete," they say, "I wasn't ready for that one!" Perhaps they aren't ready, but then birds in the field aren't exactly good at advertising their presence to give us more time to shoot at them, are they?

With a low gun position, let your puller know you are ready. He should pull each target, varying the lapse of time between each so the target appears when you least expect it. The target will appear without announcement, so as soon as you lock onto it in hard focus, that is the first beat of the rhythm.

So why is it an advantage to do it this way? Because birds don't fly in straight lines like skeet and sporting clay targets usually do. The easiest way to demonstrate this is in the field. If you see a bird approaching, point your finger at it. Regardless of the flight pattern of the bird, as it approaches, your finger will point at it with unerring accuracy. In other words, if the bird goes up or down or curls left or right, your finger will still point at it. If you now hold your arm stiffly in one position at 90 degrees to your torso, tracking the flight line of the bird will be much more difficult because you will need to develop the line of the bird by using 100 percent body movement. This is why (when we substitute the gun for the finger) developing

Polly Put the Kettle On

1. POLLY. Identify the target and slowly move the gun toward your shoulder. The muzzles of the gun start to merge on the freeway and develop the line of the bird. Lock onto the target in hard focus, and push the muzzles slightly forward and toward the line of the target. Start moving the gun slowly.

2. PUT THE. Keep lifting the gun smoothly onto the line of the target. Here the butt stock should be about halfway to your shoulder pocket. The muzzles should be moving in empathy with the bird.

3. KETTLE. Almost a completed mount, but the butt stock should still be out of your shoulder. Any deviation the bird makes can be clearly seen, and the move onto the line will be more fluid as a result.

4. ON. Here the mount is completed. As soon as the butt stock touches your shoulder, you take the shot.

the line of the bird will be much more accurate by keeping the gun out of your shoulder right up to the time the shot is triggered.

You may think that's what you always do, but after having carefully observed many bird hunters over many years I have found that is not what most of them do with a gun, even though they may think differently. Most shooters see the bird approaching, immediately mount the gun, and then track the bird all the way in. This presents all sorts of problems.

First, the view of the bird is restricted. If the approaching bird swerves or jinks left or right, you need to adjust your swing accordingly. With the gun already mounted, this isn't easy. The human torso pivots easily on a horizontal plane, more or less like a tank turret. The body always takes the easiest way to move, and inserting the butt stock into the shoulder pocket early has the effect of moving the gun in a straight line. If the bird makes any deviation from this line, a miss is inevitable. Second, the longer the gun is in your shoulder, the more you become aware of it and possibly sneak a peek at the bead or muzzles.

This is the best way to do it. Out in the field, watch the approach of the bird over the muzzles of the gun—with a fast incoming bird, this might be as much as 80 yards away. As it comes within range at about 50 to 60 yards, start your four-beat rhythm. Now it will be easy to adjust to any deviation the bird makes right up to the time you trigger the shot. With this type of shot, you always have a lot more time than you think. Use this four-beat rhythm on any bird that you can see for a long time.

So what happened to the guy that I mentioned at the start of this section, the one that loved to hunt doves but struggled because of the lack of rhythm with his shots? That weekend he went dove hunting near San Antonio. On Sunday evening, I received a text message from him. It said simply: "Polly put the kettle on, Pete! Shot lights out! Thanks for the help!" I bet I was as thrilled as he was, and that really is what it's all about, isn't it?

CHAPTER 8

Trigger-nometry

Trigonometry is a sine of the times.

—*Unknown mathematician*

Almost all bird hunters who hunt with shotguns are self-taught. Many of them also like to think that they are born with this gift from God, this "natural" ability, just like some of us like to consider that we have a great sense of humor, are fabulous lovers, or smarter than average. Most of us like to deceive ourselves, just like the gambling man who tells everyone when he wins but conveniently forgets his losses. The reason we deceive ourselves is because in bird hunting situations, unlike competitive shotgunning, no one is there to keep score.

Instinctive Shooting

Some shooting coaches will try to convince you that in hunting situations, you must always shoot all the birds instinctively. I would agree with this, but only up to a point. I am not alone in my thoughts here. The December 2001 issue of *Sporting Clays* magazine had an article by Katy Skahill about Jon Kruger, who was at the time US champion. Jon said, "I don't really believe much in instinctive clay shooting."

Coaches who specialize in the instinctive shooting method try to convince us that instinctive shotgunning is a combination of stance, posture, gun mount, and technique that allows the shot to be taken without conscious thought and without establishing a conscious relationship between the barrel and the target. That sounds great in theory, but in practice, I promise you, on some birds it won't work. Many shotgunners, especially bird hunters, are gullible, and many expect instant gratification as they learn to shoot. They like to believe that instinctive coaches will show them a magical method that will make it all so easy they will stroke fast-flying birds from the sky with a carefree abandon.

These same guys would instantly agree with the logic of the footballer who on the field must make a conscious effort to throw his ball in front of the receiver so that he can collect it smoothly. They would agree also that on the ice rink, the hockey player is instructed by his coach to "skate to the puck" as he tries to intercept it. But they believe that they can shoot right at a bird that is doing three times the speed of both the football receiver and the hockey player!

Before you disagree with me, please consider this. The laws of physics dictate that a crossing bird travelling at approximately 50 mph needs a forward allowance of approximately 3 to 4 feet at 20 yards, 5 to 6 feet at 30 yards, 8 to 9 feet at 40 yards, and 12 to 14 feet at 50 yards. If you don't learn what that looks like to you at the end of your gun, you're not going to hit many of them! We see this all the time in the field. Three mallards fly past us at about 40 yards, and we give the leading duck a barrel and stand open-mouthed as the third one drops like a stone.

The art of shooting-flying with a flintlock shotgun became fashionable in the eighteenth century. In those days, it was absolutely necessary to see lead or forward allowance of some sort because of the delay with the lock and ignition times with these early scatterguns. The muzzles needed to be positioned at an appropriate distance ahead of the target and stay there until the shot had left the barrel. In other words, the methodology in those days was an early application of the sustained lead method that is so popular and effective today.

With the shotgun, we can shoot some of the birds instinctively. For example, narrow-angle, fast-flushing birds need almost no apparent lead because the open pattern of the scattergun will, on most occasions, save the day and put another bird in the bag. In other words, you simply point the gun at the bird (just as you do with a stationary target) and the wide pattern is enough to cover the bird.

But some birds are different. With birds that are not at narrow angles and modest ranges, we need to be able to judge parallax, trajectory flight lines, and the time it takes our shot pattern to get to the target. In other words, I have yet to find anyone, in over thirty-five years as a full-time shooting coach, who can instinctively get their muzzles far enough in front of a dove crossing at 30 yards or more or, better still, a 40-yard-plus hen pheasant that comes screaming down the side of a Scottish mountain with a driving wind behind it. Simply put, you need to lead the bird, and you need to learn how far in front you need to project your shot pattern.

Throughout the history of shotgunning, champions of the instinctive methods have always periodically become popular. The legendary Annie Oakley was a supporter and proponent of the method and said in the 1880s that "shooting a shotgun is no more difficult than pointing your finger."

The theory of allowance by eye was another instinctive shooting method championed by London gunmaker Robert Churchill. I covered this methodology earlier in the shooting instruction section. Instinctive shooting has always been used by archers as a way to shoot stationary or slow moving objects with a bow and arrow. Also it has been used and taught for years by both the army and the police force as a way to shoot stationary or slowly moving targets with a handgun. In 1980, without a doubt the most successful instinctive shooting coach ever, Bobby Lamar "Lucky" Mc-Daniel, wrote a book on the subject. His techniques were classed as point shooting.

Point Shooting

As a young boy in the 1930s, McDaniel honed his instinctive techniques on his grandparents' farm in Georgia. His fame and notoriety escalated, and over the course of several years, McDaniel realized that people would pay him to learn to shoot, especially in the state of Georgia where bird hunting was a popular way to put food on the table. From 1967 to 1973, McDaniel was an instructor for the US army, where he coached soldiers in his methodology for use in jungle warfare, where a split-second point-and-shoot move was often a matter of life or death.

As I said earlier, some shots in the field, notably fast-flushing birds at narrow angles to our position, can be instinctive. Basically, this is the application of McDaniel's simple point-and-shoot principal. In addition to working for the army, McDaniel taught many thousands of bird hunters these principles, among them President Eisenhower, John Wayne, Audie Murphy, Henry Ford II, and others. Most of these guys were primarily flushing bird hunters where the lead needed to intercept them was nominal and the pattern wide enough to compensate.

To teach his methodology to others, McDaniel would demonstrate that he could hit small objects that were thrown into the air with a BB gun, which was quite an impressive feat. But there were certain things that Lucky considered to be imperative for his students to consider first, in order to make this easier for them. He preferred them to use copper-coated BBs because they sparkled in the sunlight and could be seen easier. He also selected areas that were not surrounded by trees so the students would easily see both the target object and also the sparking BB as it left the gun. The BB guns used for his lessons were also carefully modified with a weaker spring so that the flight of the BB was easily seen and picked up in flight. So although the students were never expected initially to see a conscious relationship between the

gun barrel and the target, the success of the method depended on a defined relationship between the projectile and the target. The student's ability to perceive this relationship was necessary for it to work.

Seeing the projectile's path relative to the target is nothing new. Ancient hunters did it all the time with primitive spears and arrows. When I was a kid, my friends and I all had catapults—over here you call them slingshots. We would fashion these ourselves from a suitable forked stick (cut from our fathers' privet hedge), rubber strands to power the catty cut from an old inner tube, and a pouch to hold the projectile cut from the leather tongue of one of Dad's boots. I got many a lickin' from crossing Dad and cutting gaping holes in his prized privet hedge!

Down the road from where we lived was an old canal bridge, and swallows nested underneath it. We spent hours trying to hit the birds with projectiles fired from our catapults—small rocks and pebbles, nuts, lumps of lead, or anything else that we considered suitable. Occasionally, believe it or not, we connected with one of the luckless birds and gleefully watched as our successful shot sent it tumbling bloody and bedraggled earthward.

We also rolled rusty bike wheels down the slopes of the local golf course, and like stone-age savages, threw our makeshift spears to intercept them. We became surprisingly skilled at it. But as I think back to those childhood forays, as we took aim with the slingshot—and I'm sure many of you have done the same—we always knew where the slingshot was, or where the business end of the spear was relative to the target, in our perhipheral vision. And whether the projectile was a stone, arrow, or spear, as it was released, we always looked for a nanosecond to the space in front of the target to where we wanted the intercept point to be. But let's get back to Lucky McDaniel.

McDaniel taught his students to hit steel washers that he threw into the air both vertically and horizontally. To spectators, this was an awe-inspiring, amazing feat. Just how did McDaniel accomplish this? It wasn't as difficult as you would think. Because his students could see the projected BB as it missed the target, the next shot at a similar target with a similar trajectory was easier. To get his students to hit the steel washers with any degree of success, McDaniel would instruct them to look, as they triggered each shot, not at the target, but at the appropriate space in front of it. In other words, the students learned to interpret where the target would be by the time the projectile BB would reach it.

So although the proponents of pure instinctive shotgunning insist that we should never see a conscious bird/barrel relationship, I suspect that Lucky's students did actually begin to develop an increased awareness of where their barrels were relative to each target. With lots of practice, eventually McDaniel's clients established a repertoire of bird/barrel relationships that they knew to be correct, which is exactly what we need if we are to become successful wingshooters. And this is exactly what the unit lead method (which I will explain in more detail later) will teach the aspiring bird hunter.

Learning about Lead

The BASC publication *Nontoxic Shot, Progress & Needs* (1996) contained a paper by D. W. Leeming, in which he reviewed earlier experimental aim error studies that were carried out at Nilo Farms on the effectiveness of steel versus lead shot by Kozicky and Madson in 1973 and Patuxent (Andrews and Longcore in 1969) and also the works of Australian G. Russell ("Shotgun Wounding Characteristics"). According to Leeming, total aim error is made up of two basic components:

1. Basic aim error, which is basically the shooter's ability to shoulder and point the gun at the perceived aim point. In other words, his mechanics.

2. Lead error, which is in turn made up of three parts:
   - The ability of the shooter to judge the range and flight path of the bird.
   - The shooter's knowledge of the lead requirement.
   - The shooter's ability to apply this lead.

He concluded that most misses occur because of poor form and downright bad shotgunning. In other words, exactly the result of what I have always called "poking and hoping," "poking and praying," or "praying and spraying." Make no mistake, shotgunners have always had their pet names for downright poor shotgunning. Most have no idea why they missed, and they joke about missing as though it doesn't really matter. But if most of them were to admit it, they would like to improve . . . and there is a way that they can.

For most coaches, and also shooting writers, the subject of lead is strictly taboo; it is a subject that they refuse to approach head-on. According to them, applying the correct amount of lead to the rapidly accelerating bird is something that just happens instinctively without thought, a magical process that results from meditation or burning candles. Unfortunately for most of us, that just isn't the case. Anyone who makes his living from coaching others knows this. The young student who continues to miss the crossing shot several feet behind on the skeet field until you tell him to miss the next target by 3 feet in front is open-mouthed as he does this and his next shot smacks the target squarely in the middle.

If he is a good student, he will learn from the experience and file the picture, or bird/barrel relationship, in his memory bank. With the next target he will insert the gun in the correct place, rewind the mental image, and break that target also. It wasn't instinct because someone needed to show him where that interception point was. I prefer to substitute "intuition."

In a nutshell, we miss birds because of plain ol' pilot error; we just don't know where to insert the gun relative to the target. Lead requirement is made up of speed, angle, and range. The shooter's ability to decipher these variables and fit the pieces of the mental puzzle together solves the puzzle. In other words, regardless of what others may tell you, successfully and efficiently using a shotgun isn't instinct, you need to learn how to do it. And the head-scratching part for all of us, initially, is the lead requirement.

Many shooting coaches will explain in great detail how you should fit your shotgun. They will also tell you how to mount and swing it efficiently. But unfortunately that is where the story ends. On the subject of lead these coaches tell you to "move the gun ahead of the bird until the correct sight picture is seen." Or, "Your eyes will tell you when the picture looks right to you." I agree. But only when you have preprogrammed your onboard computer to recognize which specific sight picture looks right to you, not before. The conversation on the skeet field would sound something like this.

"You missed that one behind," says your confident coach, peering over your shoulder. "Yep! That's where most of 'em go," he continues, smiling smugly. "Give it more lead."

OK, you think. *Thanks for the advice, coach.*

"So exactly how far ahead do I need to lead this bird—2 feet, 3 feet, 6 feet, perhaps 10 feet?" you ask him.

"Aha!" replies your intrepid shooting coach with a nod and a wink, "I can't tell you that. It's just a feeling. It's instinct."

Unfortunately for you, if your coach can't tell you in simple terms just how far ahead of the bird you should be as you trigger the shot, then how does he expect you to know? Comments like this have always mystified me; if your coach can't tell you how much lead to give a target, then why pay him large sums of money for shooting lessons?

"Shooting a shotgun is like pointing your finger," your coach continues. "Allow your hands to guide your eyes to the target. The shotgun gun is just an extension of your hands."

I agree. Shotguns must be pointed. But if we continually point the shotgun at the target every time, without consciously applying lead of any sort, as so many of these coaches suggest, I'm afraid we're not going to hit many of the targets.

"Allow the magic of your subconscious to tell you where to put the muzzles," your coach continues, with another nod and wink.

"This time focus really hard on the target, and your brain will tell you how much lead you need to give it," the guru continues. As you continue the lesson, your shotgun, with its wide, forgiving pattern, compensates, and by the law of averages, you manage to hit a few targets. But for the life of you, you don't know why.

Intense focus on the target does not make you shoot farther in front of it. All the intense focus does is ensure that your pellets arrive somewhere in the vicinity of the target, which may not be the appropriate distance ahead of it, and you may miss. Now, there is no easy way to say this. The main reason most coaches can't tell you how to correct the shot and give the target more lead is because they don't know how to explain it. In fact, most coaches can't. And here another surprise: Applying the correct lead, no matter what your coach tells you, isn't instinct, it is intuition.

Here's a story about a dove hunter. Let's say that somewhere in the Texas panhandle there is a young twelve-year-old named Johnny who loves to hunt doves. He inherits an old Mossberg pump from Grandpappy and can't wait for dove season each year. In the evenings, his favorite pastime after school is sitting in one of the flight lines near the waterhole and shooting doves as they cross the cow pasture on their way to roost.

At first, he succeeds merely by chance; he swings the gun with gay abandon, and if a bird happens to succumb to his erratic poke-and-hope shots, so be it. He doesn't care; he's as happy as an exuberant child opening presents on Christmas morning. But after a few outings, some of these more successful shots are etched indelibly into his hard drive. Each season he rewinds them. He begins to learn that if he puts the muzzles of his gun in front of a dove, at this angle and this range, he has a good chance of hitting it. He may not realize it at the time, but every time he pulls the trigger, regardless of if he is successful or not, he is practicing.

By the time Johnny is twenty, he is an accomplished shot. Just before the start of dove season, as he strolls into the hardware store to buy his shells, shoppers nudge each other and refer to him in hushed tones. He never forgets what he learns, and by the time he is fifty, he is an expert in the dove fields.

Is his shotgunning instinctive, or is it intuitive? In other words, over a period of time, did he learn how to do it? The answer is clear.

I don't believe there is such a thing as a natural shot. I believe some of us may be marginally better at it initially, just as some of us can run faster, jump higher, or throw stones farther than the rest. But that, in my opinion, is as far as it goes. Most bird hunters are self-taught, never pick the gun up in between seasons, and suffer from some sort of psychosis when it comes to taking instruction. Because of this, the percentage of really good shots is low. I believe that there are only two ways we become accomplished with a shotgun. The first way is to shoot thousands of rounds over a period of many years as Johnny did. The second is a shortcut, taking lessons and learning from a good instructor. Most wingshooters, if they have the choice and they would like to improve, will opt for the second. More often than not, the stumbling block for them is the lead requirement they need on the birds.

Let's imagine at this stage that you have followed my advice on eye dominance and you are absolutely positive that the eye above the rib of your shotgun is the one your brain uses to decide

when you must trigger the shots. Let's imagine also that you have practiced your gun mount and swing with due diligence and you are confident that you can move your gun with perfect empathy on any bird that flies. What is the one gray area left? Most shooters say how much lead the birds need.

Shotgunning is irrefutably a hand-eye coordination sport, much like tennis, cricket, or baseball. But there are two differences. The high speed of the shot requires you to adjust your timing, and because the bird or target is moving, you never shoot directly at it. You must place your shot charge into the anticipated flight path. Simply put, you must give the target some forward allowance or lead. The problem arises in deciding visually just how far in front that must be to ensure perfect interception. For most of us, forward allowance or lead requirement is the most baffling part of the successful shotgunning equation, but it doesn't need to be.

As I said earlier, lead is made up of three components: speed, range, and angle. Of these three, the component that influences lead requirement more than any other is the angle. If we can quickly identify the angle that the bird is flying at, we can identify the lead we need to apply to it for successful interception.

Developing the Line of the Bird

You might be familiar with the concept of visualizing a clock face to help develop the line of the bird. With this method, you imagine the bird flying across a giant clock hanging on a wall. If you move the gun too fast and in an uncontrolled swing, it will move horizontally and you'll shoot over the top of the birds; but if you visualize the bird flying across the clock face, you can develop the line better. (See the examples in the illustrations on page 77 and 78.) Later in this chapter I'll explain another way to use the clock face by visualizing it lying flat on the ground to interpret the angle of a bird.

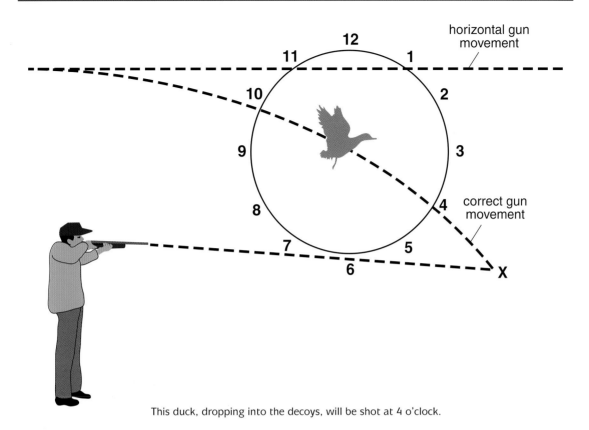

This duck, dropping into the decoys, will be shot at 4 o'clock.

Gauging Lead

Some years ago I came up with a method for applying the correct amount of lead to each target that works very well. I call it the unit lead system, and it has been tried and tested on the sporting clay course. It works just as well as a learning tool for bird hunters, and it will help you build a repertoire of sight pictures quicker than any other method. The following section will give you a clearer understanding of lead and eventually a more intuitive way to adopt and apply it in bird hunting situations.

Wingshooters—sometimes even fairly competent, experienced wingshooters—are always surprised at how much lead they need, but it's easy to demonstrate on a skeet field. The game of skeet was invented by two enterprising hunters as a way to hone their bird hunting skills in the close sea-

son. On a skeet field you learn how to accurately interpret the two main components of forward allowance, the range of the target and its angle.

The two houses on a skeet field (high and low) are exactly 40 yards apart, and the crossing point of the targets is about 20 yards (21 to be exact). The semicircular walkway around the skeet field is about 21 yards in diameter. Skeet targets travel at about 40 to 50 miles per hour. This is more or less as fast as many game birds in full flight. Now I know that fast-flying birds are not shot by making calculations with a slide rule and attempting to figure out where to put your shot charge relative to them. The following calculations do initially raise eyebrows with most of my clients, but there is absolutely no doubt in my mind that it helps most of them visually determine where this interception point should be.

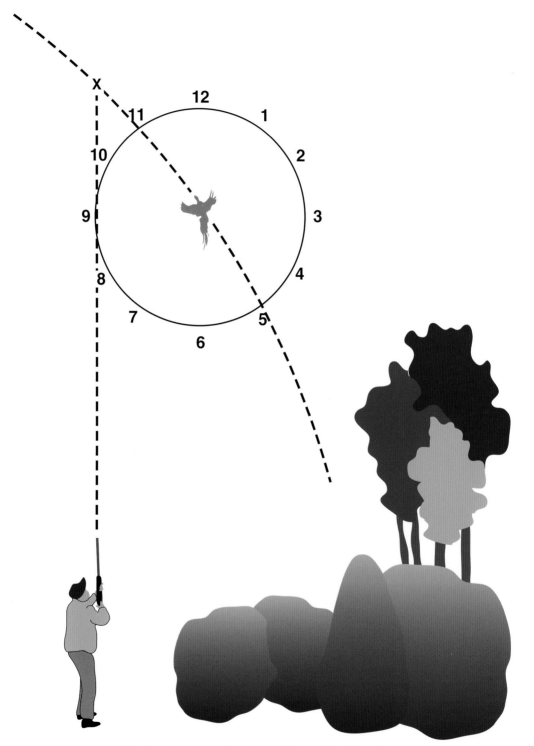

This incoming pheasant or dove will be an 11 o'clock shot.

Let's say we have a full crossing target at approximately 20 yards doing approximately 45 to 50 mph. The shot pattern from a standard shell is approximately 1,200 feet per second, which is 800 mph. That's a ration of 16:1, for every 16 yards the pellets travel toward the target, the target (or bird) will fly 3 or 4 feet in the same time interval. At an approximate range of 20 yards, you will need to place your shot pattern approximately 4 feet in front of a bird as he crosses in front of you. Due to the exponential effect of the shot charge slowing down, the lead on the same bird at 30 yards would be about 6 feet, at 40 yards about 9 feet, and at 50 yards about 12 feet. Because of this exponential effect, the distance you must shoot in front of any target becomes more difficult as range increases. Try telling a pheasant hunter standing in a Kansas cornfield that the rooster (that everyone has already shot at) now crossing in front of him at a distance of 40 yards needs an 8- or 9-foot lead, and he won't believe you.

As you trigger a shot, you need to be able to see this elusive component of lead in one of two places, either out there at the bird or target, which is difficult, or at the muzzle of the gun, which is a lot easier. It's easier to see lead at the muzzle rather than out there at the target because of the phenomenon of perspective. Perspective is our ability to judge spatial relationships at a distance. I use a simple demonstration to show this concept.

Place two orange traffic cones (or two sticks) about 6 feet apart in the middle of a field at a distance of about 50 to 60 yards. The field must be boringly flat and uninteresting, without fences, gates, and so on. The middle of a football field is perfect. Then ask several guys to glance at the traffic cones for about five seconds. Now ask the guys to each write down how far apart they think the cones are. My guess is that the results will be wildly conflicting.

If you put something that they can readily relate to next to the cones—a vehicle, safety cage, or gun rack, for example—it will be easy to make a comparison to this object and the answers will be more accurate.

One point worth mentioning here is the fact that high-velocity shells may seem like an attractive option, but the advantage of seeing less lead by using more shell on a distant target is almost inconsequential. Why? Because the pellets from a faster shell may have a slight advantage in the early stages, but although the pellets may start out faster initially, they also slow down quicker due to increased air resistance. The advantage of using these shells may be about 4 inches on a crossing bird at 40 yards, but only an inch or so on a narrow-angle shot at the same distance. The tradeoff is the increased recoil.

Unit Lead

During the years that I have been a shooting coach, I have done a great deal of research into lead in hopes of finding ways that will make it easier for shotgunners to apply lead and either break more targets or put more birds in their bags. Eventually, I came up with the unit lead method

This is an indication of what a 1-unit lead looks like at the muzzles.

This is the amount of lead you need on a full crossing target at 90 degrees to your shooting position at 20 yards. When the target is at the right-hand side of the piece of wood, you need to place your pattern at the left side.

This is the lead you need on the same target at a narrow angle.

in which you see units at the muzzle (without looking at the muzzle) instead of at the target. A unit is approximately three-quarters of an inch or the width of a one-cent piece.

Three-quarters of an inch is the only measurement that will correlate accurately into leads in feet out at the target. A one-inch increment will not work, and neither will a half-inch increment. It took me several years of documentation, experimentation, and calculation before I eventually perfected the method, and it works very well.

Let's assume that you use a standard shell of approximately 1,200 to 1,250 feet per second. If you have a 30-yard, full crossing target that comes off the throwing plate of an automatic target launcher at 40 mph (58.66 feet per second), the shot column will take 0.06 seconds to get to the target (using $7^{1}/_{2}$ shot), which means that the lead required will be approximately 5 feet, 8 inches. At the muzzles, this looks like approximately 3 inches. If we divide this by 4 we get 0.75 inch.

This three-quarters of an inch measurement at the gun end doesn't need to be exact; it's just a brief, visual indication as you make your move to intercept the target, between the side of the muzzle and the target as you trigger the shot. This is the only measurement that will work. One inch does not work, neither does a half inch.

When I first introduced this method, it was frowned upon. But the success of the method gathered momentum, especially with competitive sporting clay shooters. Today it is recognized as the best way to build up a library of sight pictures that you know to be correct. Once you get used to applying it, it becomes remarkably easy, especially for correlating the leads on longer shots.

But shooters are still skeptical, so in order to better understand how this method works so successfully, let's do some calculations. The time of flight it takes a $7^{1}/_{2}$ shot shell with an initial muzzle velocity of 1,200 to 1,250 feet per second to travel certain distances is as follows:

10 yards	0.027 second
20 yards	0.060 second
30 yards	0.097 second
40 yards	0.139 second
50 yards	0.186 second
60 yards	0.238 second

Many birds fly at speeds between 30 and 50 mph. If we calculate for a bird that is moving at approximately 30 mph, the actual lead requirement to intercept that bird with a column of $7^{1}/_{2}$ shot on a full crossing shot is 2.64 feet at 20 yards, 4.62 feet at 30 yards, and 5.56 feet at 40 yards. On a 40 mph bird, the lead is 3.52 feet at 20 yards, 5.69 feet at 30 yards, and 8.15 feet at 40 yards. The 50 mph bird needs 4.39 feet of lead at 20 yards, 7.11 feet at 30 yards, and 10.192 at 40 yards.

In bird hunting situations in the field you can't be as specific as this, and you can't calculate actual accurate linear lead measurements on live targets.

Recently someone came up with a computer program that accurately calculates the precise lead you need to see at various angles and distances using shells of various velocities. The problem is that this and other "foolproof" methods of calculating lead don't work because of the human element. The shooter still needs to evaluate range. He also needs to evaluate the angle. He also needs to evaluate the speed of the bird. These things only come from experience out in the field.

Also, a bird that you estimate is crossing in front of you at 20 yards is never going to be exactly 20 yards away. The 40 mph bird is never going to be moving at exactly 40 mph. Although you may try to shoot these targets with a sustained or constant lead method, gun speed also will vary slightly. The speed of the shot and the speed of the quarry are variables that you have very little control over, but remember also that the shotgun is a forgiving weapon. You always have a small advantage with the shot string on the close targets and a large advantage with the width of the pattern.

Simply, if you take a bird that is a full crossing shot (90 degrees to the shooter), approximate lead would be 3.5 feet at 20 yards; 5.5 feet at 30 yards; 8.5 feet at 40 yards; 11 feet, 10 inches at 50 yards; and 14 feet, 5 inches at 60 yards. Practical applications, combined with research in the field, has proved these lead requirements to be realistically accurate for our purposes.

From the calculations above you can see that on a full crossing shot, because the shot charge is slowing down rapidly as the range increases, the 40-yard target (at 40 mph) doesn't need twice the lead as the 20 yard target, but more than this. A 60-yard shot at 40 mph needs, not 10.5 feet (three times the lead assumed for the 20-yard shot), but approximately 14 feet, 5 inches of lead, over four times the lead that the 20-yard target needed. This is because the shot charge that starts off at approximately 1,200 feet per second takes about 0.06 seconds to travel 20 yards; 0.097 seconds to travel 30 yards, and 0.139 seconds to travel 40 yards and four times as long to get to the 60-yard target. The shot column simply takes longer to get there. The lead requirement doesn't increase linearly; it is exponential.

As range increases and the exponential effect comes into play, the familiar constant angle we can apply to many of the close shots is no longer adequate. This is why, on the full crossing shots, the ability to judge range is more important. If the effect of range slows the shot down considerably, as the bird gets farther away from us, we must apply more and more lead to connect with it. However, for angle targets, other than full crossers, this does not mean (as most of us would suspect) that this will proportionally increase visually by very much at the gun end, so the effect of perspective is minimized. Long shots in the field (at ducks, geese, and some driven pheasants) of up to 50 yards are by no means uncommon, and this is where, for many of us, the application of lead becomes more complicated. But it doesn't need to be if you use this system.

First of all, let's look at the difference between perceived and actual lead. We established that we need about 4 feet of lead on a 45 mph crossing shot at 20 yards. To demonstrate this to a student, I use a piece of wood painted white placed under the flight line of the low house target at the center stake.

If you now shoot the same target from a narrow angle of about 15 degrees, you still need the same lead, but the perceived lead will be a lot less, about a foot. On this 20-yard target, the lead you need to see at the muzzle is about a 1-unit lead.

But here's something that's really interesting. On the same target at the same angle at 50 yards, you can still break the target with a 1-unit lead. Why? Because the lead you need to see out there at the target is now about 3 feet or more, but the lead at the muzzle is still only about 0.9 inch, so the one unit would still work because our pattern (about 30 inches wide) will be more than enough to compensate. It sounds too good to be true, doesn't it? This means that the pheasant that jumps from the cornfield and needs a small amount of perceived lead at the muzzle at 20 yards still visually needs the same amount when he gets out to 50.

If we do some more calculations on this, a narrow-angle target, at approximately 15 degrees to our shooting position, requires the following lead at the muzzle:

Distance to the target	Lead seen at the muzzle
20 yards	0.7 inch
30 yards	0.8 inch
40 yards	0.8 inch
50 yards	0.9 inch

The actual lead we need to successfully intercept the target (not the perceived lead) may be anything from 3 feet, 6 inches on the 20-yard target to nearly 12 feet, 4 inches on the 50-yard shot. Because of the narrow angle, the perceived lead will be approximately 2 feet, 6 inches on the 20-yard target to 3 feet, 8 inches on the 50-yard shot. But the difference in the lead requirement at the muzzle between the 20-yard and the 50-yard target is only two-tenths of an inch. Does this mean that if we give any target that is either incoming or outgoing a bird/barrel relationship at the muzzle of somewhere between 0.7 inch to 0.9 inch we should connect with the bird? As amazing as this seems, that is correct. It also means that because of the beneficial effect of the width of our shot column, we can apply a specific measurement at the muzzles that would work on all the narrow-angle shots (either incoming or outgoing), and because of this, the process of applying lead is simplified.

This is true on the narrow-angle shots, but what about a wide-angle shot at, say, approximately 45 degrees to the shooter? Once again, one bird/barrel relationship on this target still works, providing we make a good interpretation of the angle of the target relative to our shooting position. If we do the calculations on this target, the lead seen at the muzzles is as follows:

Distance to the target	Lead seen at the muzzle
20 yards	1.9 inches
30 yards	2.1 inches
40 yards	2.3 inches
50 yards	2.5 inches

As the range increases, so does the lead requirement, and in order to successfully intercept this particular target, the actual lead you need is from approximately 2 feet, 4 inches on the 20-yard shot to 10 feet, 2 inches on the 50-yard shot, a difference of about 8 feet. But the difference at the muzzle is only 0.8 inch between the 20-yard and 50-yard shots because the lead at the muzzle is from approximately 1.9 inches for the 20-yard shot to 2.25 inches for the 50-yard shot. Once again, due to the width of your pattern (approxi-

mately 30 inches wide at 50 yards with an improved modified choke), you can apply a specific amount of lead at the muzzle (in this case, 3 units) that would allow you to break any target at an approximate 45-degree angle to your shooting position at any range out to 50 yards.

Remember that the lead on a clay target that flies at 40 mph is exactly the same as the duck that flies at the same speed. If you improve your skills in this way, you will see a massive advantage when you venture into the field with live quarry.

The Six Sight Pictures You Need to Know

Now the next part may surprise you. By using this unit system of visualizing lead at the muzzles (providing you make a reasonably good interpretation of the approximate angle and decide what category the target falls into before you shoot it), there are only six bird/barrel relationship lead pictures for every target presentation you find on a sporting clay course with a standard lead requirement out to about 50 yards.

How can that be? Let's say you have a target that is quartering away. The machine is to your left, and the target is from 7 o'clock to 12 o'clock, or a narrow-angle target at about 15 degrees to your shooting position. The area you intend to break this target is about 20 yards away. At 20 yards the calculations show that this target will need a visual lead of approximately 0.7 inch at the barrel. One unit is about 0.75. By using a sustained lead method, if you give this target 1 unit of lead, the target will break. If you then back up 10 yards and shoot this same target at the same angle at 30 yards, you will still break it with a 1-unit lead. (The calculations show that this target will need 0.8 inches of lead.) And you'll break the same target with 1 unit out to 40 yards and farther.

If the target in the area you intend to shoot is quartering in at an approximate angle of 15 degrees to your shooting position, the lead will still be 1 unit. Another amazing thing is that on these incoming or outgoing angled shots making a conscious evaluation of range isn't necessary. So if you give an incoming target that is coming toward you at a narrow angle (for example, a low #1 on a skeet field) a 1-unit lead at the muzzle, the target will break. If you give another target at the same angle to your shooting position, but coming from a high tower that is 50 yards away, a 1-unit lead at the muzzle, this target will also break.

Think of the spokes on a bicycle wheel. Imagine you are standing in the center of a wheel and draw two imaginary lines, one from the pupil of your master eye (or the eye above the rib) and the other along the rib of the gun out to the target. The amount of lead increases proportionally at the target end as the range increases. This means, in effect, that if you give a narrow-angle target a small amount of lead at the muzzles, the lead at the target will increase more substantially as a result. You can see from the diagram that you don't need to substantially increase the visual lead at the gun end on these angled shots.

I should point out that if the target is farther away, then mathematically you need more lead to intercept it. That is *mathematically* correct, but *visually*—in other words, the amount of gap you need to see at the muzzles of the gun—1 unit still works on these narrow-angle targets. As the target or bird gets farther away, the angular lead will visually remain more or less the same.

Now let's do the calculations on the lead for an intermediate-angle target that is going out at approximately 8 o'clock to 12 o'clock, or at approximately 30 degrees to your shooting position. The calculations show that you need approximately 1 foot, 9 inches of lead if you shoot this target with a shell with a velocity of 1,200 feet per second. The lead seen in inches at the muzzle is about 1.4 inches. If you apply the unit lead method to this target, you need 2 units or approximately 1.5 inches.

Don't forget that on this target your shot pattern is about 24 to 30 inches, so if you shoot the target with 2 units of lead at the muzzle, it should break. Once again, if you shoot this same target at the same angle but now at 30 yards, the calculations show that you need 2 feet, 10 inches, but at the muzzle you see 1.5 inches, exactly 2 units. At 40 yards, the calculations show 4 feet, 2 inches at the target but about 1.7 inches at the gun. Once again the 2-unit lead works.

Now look at the same target at 50 yards. The figures show that you need 7 feet, 5 inches of lead out there at the target, but at the muzzle end you only need 2 inches—a very modest increase of half an inch. But at the gun end due to the combination of the bike wheel effect and pattern, the 2-unit lead still works on this target.

A wide-angle shot is going out at somewhere between 9 o'clock and 10 o'clock to 12 o'clock, or approximately 45 to 60 degrees to your position. To shoot this target at this angle, the lead you need to see at the muzzles is about 1.9 inches. For the same target at 60 degrees, you need about 2.3 inches of lead. The average of the two is 2.1 inches at the muzzle. Using the unit lead system, you need to give this target about 3 units. If you first shoot this target at 20 yards, the lead you need at the target end is about 2 feet, 6 inches. At the muzzle, it is approximately 2 inches. A 3-unit lead is about 2.25 inches (0.75 x 3), so you should break the target with a 3-unit lead. Once again, if you shoot this same target at 30, 40, 50 yards, and farther, the 3 units still work as the target gets farther away. The calculations at 50 yards show lead at the target is approximately 10 feet, 6 inches at the same angle, and the 3-unit lead still works. It may sound too good to be true, but this method does work.

If you can apply both 1-, 2-, and 3-unit leads to the angles, what about the full crossing shots? Any target that is at an angle more than about 60 degrees to your shooting position in the area you intend to shoot it is a full crossing shot. On full crossers, you need to consider the exponential effect. This is what works on these shots:

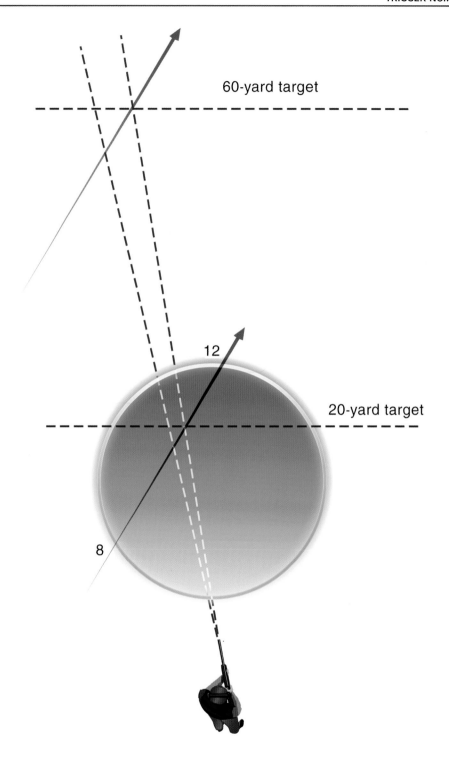

This diagram shows the lead at the muzzles on a narrow-angle shot from 20 yards out to 60 yards.

Distance to the target	Lead seen at the muzzle
20 to 30 yards	4 units
30 to 40 yards	5 units
40 to 50 yards	6 units

As I said, range and angle are the variables that have the biggest impact on the outcome of the shot (especially on full crossing shots), and because of this, a reasonably accurate assessment must be made before you take the shot. Range is difficult for most of us to judge at first, but on full crossing shots, when in doubt it is best to err on the forward side. If you are too far in front, you may still break the target with the tail end of your shot column. If you are a millionth of an inch behind the target, you will miss.

Interpreting the Bird's Angle

Learning to apply the unit lead method to your bird hunting situations is relatively easy; the secret is developing your ability to identify the angle that the bird is flying along relative to your shooting position.

If you can make a quick interpretation of the angle of the bird relative to your position, you have a pretty good chance of intercepting it. By visualizing a clock face lying on the ground in front of you, you can quickly learn the angles and perceived leads you need.

If you imagine you are always standing at 6 o'clock on the clock face, directly opposite is 12 o'clock. The bird that flies away from you from left to right along an approximate line of 7 o'clock to 12 o' clock is a narrow-angle shot, and it requires an approximate 1-unit lead at the muzzle. I must stress that this is just a brief, visual indication. You must never look back at the gun to measure this in relation to your muzzles. The muzzles must remain in your perhiphery.

The pictures on page 88 show what these units look like at the end of the gun. A 6-unit lead is approximately 4.5 to 5 inches at the muzzle. But I must stress that this is only a brief visual indication that you must apply without looking at the gun. The muzzles must remain at all times in your periphery.

To get back to the method, the target that flies from right to left at 5 o'clock to 12 o'clock would need 1 unit, 4 o'clock to 12 o'clock 2 units, and 3 o'clock to 12 o'clock 3 units. The full crosser from 3 o'clock to 9 o'clock requires 4 units. In order to learn how to apply this in the field, most of us would first benefit by shooting a few targets on a skeet field to become familiar with these bird/barrel relationships before we venture into the field.

This is how to do it: Stand at station one. You are standing at 6 o'clock, and the low house window is directly in front at 12 o'clock. If you pull a target, you will see it coming toward you at an angle of about 15 degrees, or approximately 7 o'clock. The lead you need on this target is 1 unit.

Shoot the targets initially with one eye. For example, if you are a right-shouldered, two-eyed shooter, close your left eye. Eye dominance is far more complicated than we imagine. By using only one eye, you see a crystal-clear bird/barrel relationship showing what you need to break the target convincingly.

To break this target, move your gun smoothly onto the line, and as soon as the target is about the width of a penny from the side of the barrel, pull the trigger. Do not look at the end of the barrel. The barrel must always remain in your periphery. Do this several times until you have filed this bird/barrel relationship away in your hard drive. Then you can shoot the same target again with two eyes. Is the lead picture better or worse? Some find that with both eyes open, because of strong right-eye dominance, the picture will remain the same and the target will break. But some find that now, because of less strong dominance, the ghost image of your barrel in your periphery is unclear,

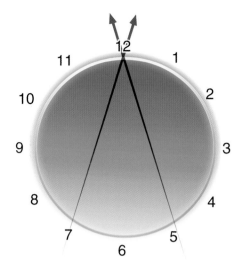

A narrow-angle shot requires a 1-unit lead.

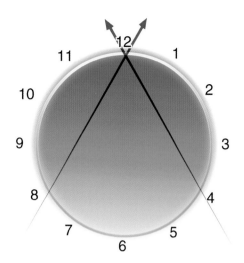

A shot from 8 o'clock to 12 o'clock requires a 2-unit lead.

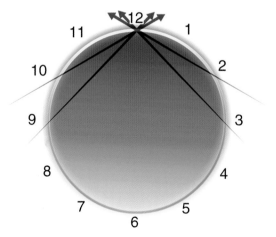

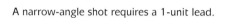

A shot from 9 o'clock to 12 o'clock requires a 3-unit lead.

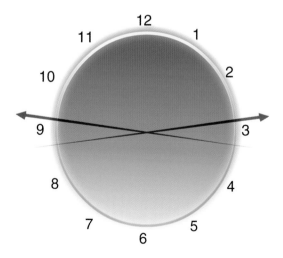

A full crosser requires a 4-unit lead.

Sight Pictures for the Unit Lead System

1-UNIT LEAD. This is the visual indication of a 1-unit lead at the muzzles.

2-UNIT LEAD. If the angle is increased slightly and the line is now 8 o'clock to 12 o'clock, a 2-unit lead would work.

3-UNIT LEAD. Increase the angle again to 9 o'clock to 12 o'clock and a 3-unit lead will work.

4-UNIT LEAD. The bird flying from 9 o'clock to 3 o' clock, crossing at approximately 90 degrees to your shooting position, requires a 4-unit lead at 20 to 30 yards.

5-UNIT LEAD. This is a 5-unit lead at 30 to 40 yards.

6-UNIT LEAD. This is a 6-unit lead at 40 to 50 yards.

and the target flies on unscathed. Close the off eye to see if the bird/barrel relationship becomes clearer and the target is hit.

Now let's shoot a target that is quartering away at narrow angle. Go to station six on the skeet field. Think of the clock face again—now the same target is at a narrow angle at approximately 15 degrees going away from you, or at approximately 5 o'clock to 12 o'clock. The same sight picture that you used on station one, with the target approximately a penny width from the side of your gun, works on this target.

Your brain is like a computer, easily capable of evaluating these angular variables, but you must first feed information in to program your hard drive. As your brain becomes programmed with these units of lead on the skeet field or sporting clay course, the sight pictures you learn there will apply and adapt readily to bird hunting situations in the field. Eventually, as you build up your personal repertoire of sight pictures that you know to be correct, out in the field you will subconsciously apply them to each situation.

For example, the rooster pheasant that erupts from your feet in the Kansas cornfield and powers away at a narrow angle to you will be a 1-unit lead shot for you. If that same bird curls away from you and crosses directly in front of your hunting buddy who is standing some distance away on your right at about 20 to 30 yards, the lead on the same bird for him will be 4 units. Most times, in actual bird hunting situations you have more time than you think, and you must allow your brain time to compute the variables.

CHAPTER 9

Bobs and Blues

And as I skirt the thicket hedge and through the stubble pass,

I see the bevies of the quail spring from the faded grass,

In every weedy tussock, in every swale they hide,

And as they sail o'er hedges, in winnowing far and wide,

The sportsman's heart exulteth, with promise of the joy,

When first the "open season" his gun and dog employ.

—*Isaac McLellan*

Over the last fifteen years or so I have lived in Dallas, Texas. Mention bird hunting in Texas, and only one game bird will spring to mind, the bobwhite quail. The first time I ever shot quail I was at Wildcat Mountain Ranch, located on the northern end of the Edwards Plateau near San Angelo. The ranch belongs to a good friend of mine, Tony Farris, and over the years Tony and his brothers have developed the place into one of the premier quail and deer hunting locations in Texas.

We don't have quail in Scotland, so as you can imagine, I was both excited and apprehensive when Tony first invited me. For several days before the trip, I quizzed some of the members at the Dallas Gun Club where I was the resident shooting coach. I was hoping that the members could fill me in on a few of the ramifications and pitfalls of quail hunting. The members were very helpful, but nothing any of them told me could have prepared me for the first time I experienced a covey rise.

On the day of the hunt, there were about a dozen or so other guys at the ranch, most of them, I suspected, seasoned quail hunters. Tony's younger brother Hollis was in charge of the ranch kitchen. We all ate a huge cholesterol-full breakfast washed down with hellishly strong coffee that just about managed to crawl out of the pot. Tony—a big, affable sort of guy who always reminded me of James Arness of *Gunsmoke* fame—

poured himself a cup, took a big gulp of the scalding liquid, and didn't even blink.

"You've never been on a quail hunt before, have you, Pete?" he asked, with a drawl as thick as my granny's porridge. I suspected the question was mainly for the benefit of the other guys. I had my suspicions that I was Tony's show and tell, and some of the other hunters were curious about the Scottish alien with the strange accent. I confirmed that I had never shot quail, but then, what was all fuss about? How difficult could it be? I had hunted the elusive red grouse on some of the best grouse moors in Scotland, and these were little brown birds about half the size. I was in for a rude awakening.

After breakfast we loaded the guns and dogs and then piled into our designated trucks. I was put in the front seat of a big white Chevrolet with Hollis and his two dogs, Blue and Missy, who both decided to lick and slobber over me. I didn't dare move.

"Whale hay-ull, Pete!" Hollis drawled, as he noticed what was happening, "Scooch over a tad bit, them dogs ain't had their vittles yet!" I didn't bother to ask Hollis what he meant.

The truck rattled and bounced along the unpaved ranch roads, rocks pinging off the underside assaulting our ears. It sounded like a handful of nuts and bolts trying to escape from a biscuit tin. We eventually lurched to a halt at the bottom of a weedy creek bed, and I piled out of the truck, happy to escape the attentions of the two dogs. Luckily there was no bloodshed; I had escaped with just a few lines of drying white slobber down my shirtfront. Splitting into groups, we were soon walking through some of the most hostile landscape I could imagine. The prickly pear, cholla, mesquite, and shin oak scrub were hardly inviting to my mind, but it was the ideal quail habitat, I was informed.

"Buy yourself some brush pants," I was told, and I was glad I did. "And you'll need some snake boots, lots of rattlers about this time of year." You can't beat an encounter with a poisonous snake to start the day, can you? As we covered the ground, I was momentarily attracted by the ruby red fruits on a prickly pear cactus, the first one I'd ever seen. I stupidly poked a cluster of spines on it to see if the needles were really that sharp. They were. I was pulling them out of the end of my finger for the next three days.

I shuffled along in the line trying to look as though I knew what I was doing. It was hot, almost 90 degrees. I was sweating, trying to avoid more cactus, tripping over rocks, and listening for rattlesnakes. Apart from those minor inconveniences, I was having a great time. Suddenly the dogs stiffened to a point directly in front of me. Every nerve in my body danced in anticipation, and I could hear my pulse.

"Get ready, Pete!" Tony hissed. I was looking hard at the patch of ground that had been pegged by the dogs, but I should have known better from my Scottish grouse hunting days. I was ready, or so I thought. Safety off, gun just out of my shoulder, and then the ground in front of me exploded into a blur of movement . . . and there they were.

It looked as though the explosion had detonated about a dozen clods of dirt with wings. The bursting birds seemed to get up from right under my feet and whirred noisily away like large clockwork bumblebees. My heart thudded a tattoo in my chest and then, "Boom! Boom!" I emptied my gun and watched the little beggars vanish quickly into the ample cover. "So that's what a covey rise is," I thought, as the tension dissipated. "I'll be ready for them next time!" But I wasn't.

Next time the dogs went on point, I was convinced that I would be calm and not fall apart at the seams . . . right up to the time the birds flushed from the plum thicket like russet Exocet missiles, and I was scared witless again. The covey rose perfectly in front of me, and once again, my salvo of shots spurred the birds on into the next arroyo. Of course, the seasoned quail hunters at Tony's ranch thought this was hilarious.

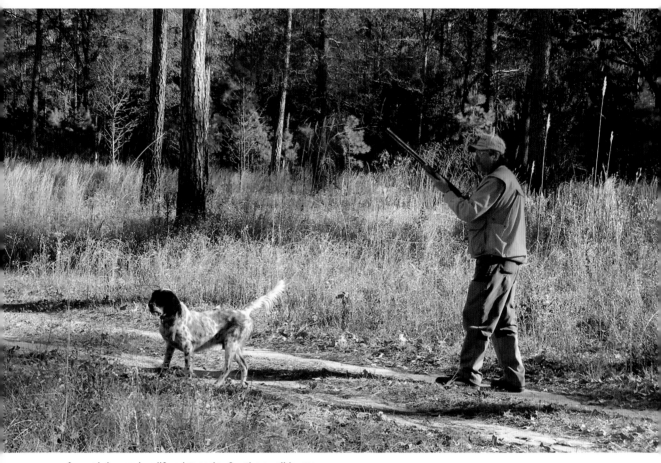

A good dog makes life a lot easier for the quail hunter. NICK SISLEY PHOTO

"It's amazing how them little birds can still fly when they're full of number eight shot, isn't it?" Hollis grinned. But I didn't rise to the bait. I started looking for excuses. At first, I blamed it on the whirring clamor of wings. But wasn't that similar to walking up unexpectedly on a rooster pheasant? Doesn't he cockle loudly as he jumps from the switch grass under your feet? I had shot many a rooster pheasant in similar situations in Scotland, and I was preprogrammed to respond to that. But that was only one bird, and here there were over a dozen or more.

Nothing I had ever shot before in Scotland compared to those fast-flushing coveys of quail at Tony's ranch that day. I know now that quail hold as tightly as a limpet on a rock at low tide, proba-

bly better than any game bird. They don't only hold to the dogs, but even as the hunters walk forward to flush them.

The early warning system for most quail hunters is the whirr of wing beats. I was missing so many because I was flock shooting instead of picking my bird. My excuse over lunch was that it was all new to me, and of course it was. But it didn't stop the embarrassment. To admit that my shooting skills on that day were pitiful was an understatement. The big-shot shooting coach from Scotland felt like an idiot wrapped in a moron.

This first episode at Tony's ranch was my introduction to quail hunting. Luckily for me, one of the perks of being a shooting coach is that you get lots of invitations to shoot at some of the premier quail hunting ranches in the South. Rather than suffering a severe case of embarrassment again, I thought it would be prudent to snap up these invitations whenever possible.

One of these places was "The Best Quail Ranch in the World," the T. Boone Pickens Mesa Vista Ranch near Pampa in the Texas panhandle. Mr. Pickens, the billionaire oil man, is a legend in his own lifetime and I felt privileged to meet him; he is an amazing guy.

A few years ago, at the age of seventy plus, Mr. Pickens stroked mourning doves, riding the thermals of the hot Texas breeze out of the sky with a confident flourish. Later that year, I watched as, with the speed of a striking rattler, he knocked a pair of bobs out of a covey as they exploded like a Thanksgiving firework from the plumb thicket and desert sage. What Mr. Pickens lacked in youth he more than made up for with experience, and

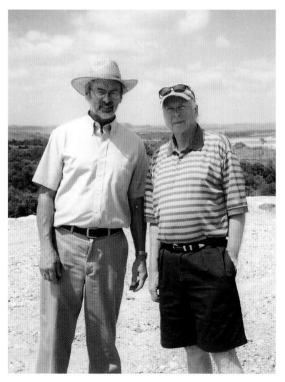

Me and the legendary Boone Pickens at Mesa Vista Ranch in the Texas panhandle.

I would have backed him any day against a guy half his age.

Over the last fifteen years or so, I have put my time in and would now consider myself a competent quail shot. Quail hunting brings out the best in me. More to the point, I have coached and improved the skills of hundreds of quail hunters, and I know what works.

Picking Your Bird

To the uninitiated, the combination of nerves frayed from the highly charged tension of the hunt and suddenly being mesmerized by the drumbeat of whirring wings from the bevy of birds is emotionally and mentally overpowering. Then the ultimate choice faces you: picking out a single bird and staying with it until you trigger the shot.

There are only two ways to learn this. The first one is to hunt lots of quail. For most of us, that may not be an option. The second way is to learn to shoot quail, or any fast-flushing bird for that matter, to a rhythm. This really works, so well in fact that I felt it deserved a complete chapter earlier in this book. I install six machine covey rise systems on many of the private ranches throughout Texas that can be loaded with different colored targets to teach quail hunters to pick one bird out at a time.

Quail don't fly as fast as their wing beats suggest. I have heard over the years that bobwhites can fly 60 mph, but this just isn't true. The southern bobwhite quail (*Colinus virginianus*) is only about nine or ten inches long and weighs about five or six ounces. Flat out he may do 40 mph, a little more with a stiff tailwind. Blues or mountain quail are larger, but even they will only be marginally faster in flight.

Quail like companionship. Coveys can have twenty or more birds in them, but the average is about a dozen or more. At night quail bunch together in a circle, and coveys smaller than seven or eight do not provide the warmth that these small birds need to survive some of the cooler night temperatures. In the morning, after the sun has

This is the covey rise system on a private ranch, a system that works extremely well to teach a hunter to shoot quail.

been up for a few hours and the dew has dried, the covey will move to an area to feed.

On the covey rise, most times the birds are only visible for about three or four seconds because good quail habitat provides them with escape cover in all directions.

Gun Position

Most quail hunters walk with their guns across their chests, and this is the normal way to walk up on the birds. The shotgun's center of gravity is close to the body, and the gun will feel lighter as a result. But if the birds flush as the gun is held in this way, as the butt comes into the shoulder pocket for the shot, the muzzles move momentar-

When hunting quail, most hunters carry their guns across their chests.

This is a better position for your gun as the dogs go on point.

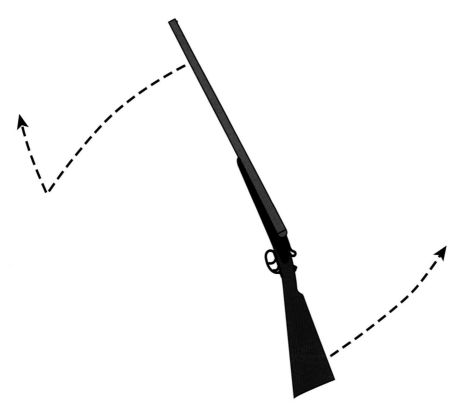

If you hold the gun across your chest as you are walking up on the birds, the muzzles will move down and then up again when you mount the gun—twice the necessary movement.

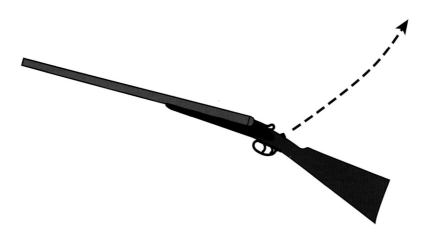

Hold the gun at a 30- to 40-degree angle as you walk. When the birds flush, you won't have to move the gun as much.

ily downward, exactly the opposite of where the rising birds in the covey are going. The muzzles will prescribe a check mark as they do this—twice the necessary gun movement. In other words, the muzzles will first move down, stop, and then start to move up again onto one of the rising birds.

There is a better way, one that is used for walking up red grouse in Scotland, and it works very well. I think the main reason hunters use it over there is that red grouse are put up at extended ranges, and to bag them you need to be on them quickly.

With quail, as the dogs go on point, hold the gun just out of your shoulder but at an angle of about 30 to 40 degrees to the horizontal. The dogs will be perfectly safe with the gun in this position. Now, as the birds flush, if you mount the gun with both arms in unison and push the muzzles forward with a slight bayonetting action (the parallel action described in chapter 4), the muzzles will lift smoothly onto the line of the bird instead of dipping down first, recovering, and then moving up again to reestablish the line. It's called economy of movement, and you will get on the bird much quicker. At the same time, as you raise the gun, you must take a short step to the bird with your leading leg in the direction that the bird is going. It doesn't take much, but as you do this, the muzzles will follow your body movement toward the bird.

You can use this method on all pointed birds over dogs. I have coached experienced quail hunters, many of whom were set in their ways, and during the course of the lessons persuaded them to try this method. A good percentage were pleased with the results.

Focusing on the Birds

When the dogs go on point, it is best not to concentrate on the ground in front of them to try to spot the birds. We have two areas of vision, peripheral or soft focus and hard focus. The human eyes

take approximately a fifth of a second to go from peripheral to hard focus. Even if we do manage to spot one or two of the birds—which is usually impossible anyway because they blend into their surroundings too well—our eyes will be locked on them in hard focus. If our eyes are already in hard focus, locked onto the birds on the ground, now they need to relax and go into soft focus, and then back into hard focus to lock onto a single bird. In other words, this will take us takes two-fifths of a second instead of one-fifth, or twice as long. With fast-flushing birds (quail especially) there is no time to waste, but you must still allow the visual input to your brain time to register.

Experienced quail hunters will be familiar with their own dogs' body language, and most pointing dogs will give you clear indication of the proximity of the birds. Watch the dog's tail closely. It will be wagging as it locates the covey, but stationary as

This quail hunter is looking above the ground, with his eyes in soft focus.

it locates and locks onto an individual bird. Look at the dog's head. If his nose is parallel to the ground, he's still unsure of the exact location of the bird. If his head is pointing in a downward direction, however, with his tail firmly locked, there is a good chance that he has located the bird precisely and the covey rise is imminent. Get ready!

Trying to focus on the birds before they flush is, I believe, one of the main reasons inexperienced quail hunters flock-shoot because as the covey flushes, their eyes are desperately trying to pick one bird out. Flock shooters never kill many quail; even when a large covey flushes, there is a lot of fresh air between birds.

Try to do it this way. Look above the ground at about head height to where the birds are expected. Now, as they flush, you will pick the covey up quickly with your peripheral vision. Peripheral vision is very sensitive to movement—to demonstrate this, stand with your arms outstretched to either side and wriggle your fingers.

On the covey rise, the birds will lift into the horizontal plane, and as they do, they will be easier to distinguish from their surroundings. Your peripheral vision will pick up rapid wing movement, and it should be easier to lock onto one bird just as the gun is coming into your shoulder.

When two hunters move in on the birds, the guy on the left takes the birds that flare left; the guy on the right takes the birds on the right. It's common sense, but it's surprising how many hunters forget this during the adrenaline rush of the rise. This isn't just a safety rule to keep the muzzles from straying in an errant direction toward the other hunter, but a matter of etiquette to prevent both hunters from shooting the same bird.

You need to step to the bird when walking behind dogs. (More about this in the pheasant hunting section.) For the right-shouldered shooter, his weight should be over his left leg as he triggers the shot. Otherwise he may be caught off balance for his first shot, and he will definitely be off balance if he gets the chance of a second!

Stand with your arms outstretched and wriggle your fingers. Even though you are looking to the front as you do this, your peripheral vision will pick up the movement of your fingers.

If you need to kick around to put the birds up, do it with your right foot so you can reposition it for a good shooting position. As the dogs go on point, always try to stop with the left leg toward the anticipated flight path of the birds. The more quail hunting you do, the more intuitive this will become. I know some experienced quail hunters who seem to know exactly where the birds will go. And here's another tip: If a quail takes a shot but he still has his head up, it is best to hit him again. If you don't, chances are that he will hit the ground running and you will lose him. This is also true of pheasants and ducks.

Equipment

If you're considering what equipment you need for quail hunting, comfortable footwear is at the top of the list. Don't buy a pair of shoes a few days before quail season and then wear them for a full

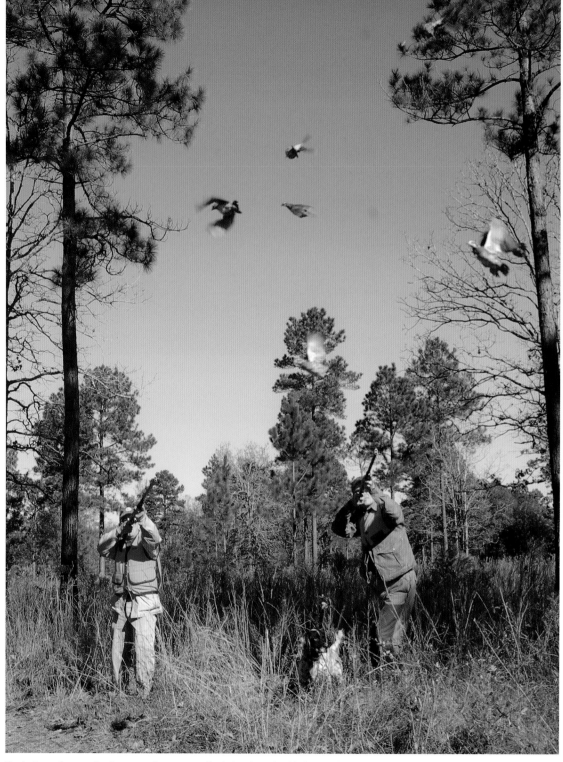

Both for safety and etiquette, the guy on the left takes the birds on his left, and the guy on the right takes the birds on the right. NICK SISLEY PHOTO

day in the blistering heat stumbling over rocky, cactus-clad ground. Shoes must be reasonably lightweight and comfortable enough to walk all day in. The tiniest blister on your foot can cause excruciating agony and completely ruin a good day's quail hunting. Although many shooters go for the jogging shoe type of hiking boot, in my opinion, these do not offer enough protection against rocks for the sides of your feet and ankles. Depending on your location, snake boots might be a good option.

Pants must be rugged enough to withstand cactus, and I prefer the nylon and canvas reinforced ones. Some shooters simply wear chaps over a pair of denims. If hunting in cool locations during the morning hours, you must have a way to transport your clothing as you remove each piece as the day gets warmer. If you put excess clothes into your game pouch, you will ruin your harvested birds.

Probably the most important thing for most of us to consider next is guns and ammunition. A quail gun needs to be responsive and quick to point. You should be familiar with the gun and be able to point it as easily as you point a finger. It needs to be fairly lightweight so that you can carry it with comfort all day. If I could carry one gun for quail, it would be a 20-gauge side-by-side.

My next choice would be a 26- or 28-inch barreled over-and-under, also 20 gauge. For most of my wingshooting, I prefer an over-and-under, but there are situations when hunting over flushing and pointing dogs where I prefer a side-by-side. This goes for quail, pheasant, woodcock, and grouse, but quail hunting is the main one.

The reasoning is twofold: First of all, most over-and-unders have the trigger selector and the safety catch on the tang behind the top lever. The selector needs to be pushed three different ways, and in the heat of a flush, a sometimes hurried operator can fumble and select neither barrel. The second

reason is that most quail (and other fast-flushing birds) can be pointed with almost no conscious lead requirement. The broad sighting plane of the two side-by-side barrels give you slightly more muzzle awareness than the narrower pointing plane

Two nice bobs taken with a 28 gauge. NICK SISLEY PHOTO

A 20 gauge is ideal for quail or dove. The type of grip you choose depends on your personal preference, and these guns show the huge variation in the style of the grip. From left to right, the first gun has a straight English stock, but with a single trigger, which is unusual. The second gun, a Parker side-by-side, also has the English grip, combined with the more usual double triggers. The third and fifth guns have full pistol grips, and the fourth has a Prince of Wales grip.

A very pretty (but expensive!) quail gun. You need a gun you can point as easily as you point your finger.

of the over-and-under. Many upland bird hunters favor the side-by-side for this reason. Most quail will be shot within three seconds of the covey rise and within 25 yards. The ammunition and choke choice are 1 ounce loads of 7^1/$_2$ or 8 shot and open chokes of either cylinder or improved cylinder. Quail are small birds; with more choke and more lead in the air than this, a direct hit would destroy the bird for the table.

Quail hunting, as I found out, is not easy. I read somewhere that statistically, an average quail hunter makes about five or six trips for an average of two birds a trip. Quail hunting is nerve-wracking, heart-stopping stuff. If your dogs work hard, you're in the right place at the right time, and you're fit enough and fast enough to get on the birds before others do, you'll maybe get one or two more. Maybe.

CHAPTER 10

Dances with Doves

Stand, swing tail, head then shoot.

Another down I take to boot.

Vision locked on point of fall.

Straight out through the grasses tall.

—*Carl Gerard*

Doves and pigeons are my favorite quarry, and for the shooting sportsman, few birds provide more challenging shots. Since I arrived in the States in 1997, I have shot my fair share of doves. Before this I often shot wood pigeons both in the south of England and the Scottish Borders. Their larger cousins, the pigeon species, present difficult targets but lack the aerial agility of the dove.

There are lots of dove and pigeon species, and some of my clients are specialist dove hunters. In Texas the mourning dove is the strong favorite, with the whitewing second. Argentina is one of the premier dove hunting locations in the world, and South America has the eared dove. The turtle dove of Africa is one of the speediest and most difficult targets, along with the rock pigeon, which frequents the cliffs of South Africa.

Like skirmishing MiG fighters in the Korean War, doves fly fast, ducking and diving with amazing aerial agility to defeat and frustrate us. With their long wings and pointed tails, they have been clocked at over 60 mph. This combination of speed and erratic dipping, diving flight behavior makes doves easy to identify but difficult to hit. But there is a way.

When I hunted doves for the first time in the US, it was near Muleshoe, Texas. The invite came out of the blue, late one Sunday night. I had been busy all day at the Dallas Gun Club, with lots of lessons in the over 100-degree temperatures as the dove hunters flocked in to hone their skills for the approaching season.

That night, I was beat. I slumped into the chair and popped the top off a welcome cold beer. It was getting late, the next day was Monday, and I was off the clock, so it didn't matter if I had a beer or three. I was into my third one, almost ready to hit the sack . . . and the phone rang. I nearly ignored it, but my wife, Alison, suggested it might be important. So I dragged my backside out of the chair to answer it. It was Larry, one of the maintenance guys at the Dallas Gun Club.

"You ever been dove hunting?" he asked. "I meant to invite you before now, but I forgot. My folks have a place near Lubbock. Lots of doves about this year—you should come."

It was almost 10:30 p.m. I had been at the gun club all day, and Larry had driven past the skeet field where I was coaching at least twenty times and never mentioned the possibility of a dove hunting trip. But you know the feeling. For the hunting man, the anticipation of a good hunt always overtakes any feeling of tiredness. Larry agreed to pick me up at 8 in the morning, and I rolled wearily into the sack.

The next morning, my numb brain registered the sound of the alarm in the distance, but I dozed off again. Alison woke me up with a shake on the shoulder and an order.

"There's a big gray truck parked outside; you'd better see who it is."

I was hanging on the edge of consciousness, but somewhere in the distance, I remembered the dove hunting trip. The thought spurred me into groggy action. I blearily peered out the bedroom window, and Larry gave me a hearty wave.

I hastily got dressed and went downstairs to where Alison made some breakfast and strong coffee. I needed the coffee, but I swallowed the scrambled eggs and toast without really tasting them. Reaching for the half-empty coffee mug, I stood up to deal with the more important things for the trip. Larry poured himself some coffee and then followed me into the garage as I hunted for my gear. I unlocked my gun safe and selected a Browning 20 gauge and a few boxes of shells. Larry noticed that I only reached for a couple of boxes.

"Two boxes?" Larry commented quizzically, then added, "You got cammo?" I shook my head no in return. I never needed it except for my duck hunts, and thick thermal jackets and waders didn't seem like appropriate attire for 100 degrees or more in the Texas desert.

"You'll need some. Wally's is on the way, so we'll stop there." Wally's? I didn't ask.

We hit the painfully frustrating bumper-to-bumper traffic as we merged onto I-35. Back then, I wasn't used to the Texas roads and the antics of American drivers who, during the early morning commute, assume the role of the kamikaze pilot. I swear that some of these drivers are still half asleep. The ones who are awake are often preoccupied with other mundane tasks, but driving a vehicle at 65 miles an hour in heavy traffic isn't one of them. For the women, this is makeover time. With practice, they can deftly apply their makeup as they drive with both hands off the steering wheel.

Two nice doves harvested from a field of sunflowers. NICK SISLEY PHOTO

But I was getting used to it. We eventually made it through the morning madness and headed along I-20 through Fort Worth toward Abilene. I remembered Abilene from my teenage folk-singing-in-pubs days.

"Abilene, Abilene, prettiest town I've ever seen," as the song goes. I didn't agree.

"Only another 70 miles and we'll be in Lubbock," Larry informed me cheerfully. "There's a Wally's there. We'll get you a dove license and some camo."

I stifled a groan. Another 70 miles and we'll only be in Lubbock, I think. Unlike Scotland, Texas roads are usually constructed in perfect, laser-straight lines wherever possible. Nothing like a road that appears to stretch into oblivion to make you feel as though you're going nowhere. They get you there quicker, admittedly, but there is a price to pay—absolute boredom.

We eventually drove into Lubbock and stopped at Walmart. This is Wally's, I thought. I bought a camo hat, shirt, gloves, pants, a dove license, and at Larry's suggestion, a few more boxes of 20-gauge shells.

"Buddy Holly was born here," Larry told me as we walked back to the truck. I liked that. Buddy Holly was a favorite of mine from my younger days, and sure enough, there was a big memorial to him in the center of the town. Unfortunately, Larry annoyingly hummed "Peggy Sue" in my right ear for the next 20 miles.

The remainder of the journey was mile after mile of flat and almost featureless landscape, without a hint of elevation until we reached the endless swaying seas of milo, millet, cotton, and nodding giant yellow sunflowers surrounding the infant town of Muleshoe. Now this was interesting. I had never seen a landscape like it before. The fields of

Dove country.

sunflowers were nothing short of awe inspiring, seas of gently swaying burnt gold as far as the eye could see. I knew doves loved sunflowers and millet. This, I was convinced, was dove nirvana.

I almost licked my lips in the anticipation of what I expected to unfold that morning. And yet, pangs of doubt gnawed at the back of my mind. As I eagerly scanned the distant horizon for flocks of doves, apart from the odd lonesome one drifting lazily along in the shimmering haze, I was disappointed. Perhaps a cold front had come through that we had not heard about and scattered the birds? The thought worried me.

The impact of mechanization over the last few decades had left its mark on the vast plains of West Texas. Small farms had grown into medium-sized farms, which had in turn blossomed into bigger farms. But as always, progress has its price, and the area was not without casualties. Empty shacks, which had once sheltered hardworking but happy families, scarred the landscape, sad reminders of a bygone era. Each house had its attendant stand of elm trees, planted presumably to offer the occupants some respite from the searing heat of the Texas sun.

Red dirt roads crisscrossed the landscape, and at the end of one of them, hidden behind a stand of these ancient elms, was the small house and barn belonging to Larry's parents. As we pulled into the yard at the rear of the house, we were greeted by Larry's brother-in-law Gary and what appeared to me to be a pack of starving dogs.

Larry's truck crunched to a halt, and he jumped out to greet his in-law. After the usual exchange of pleasantries, Gary turned to me.

"Howdy! So you're the shooting instructor guy from Scotland," he said. "You bring plenty of shells?"

"Couple of boxes of number 8s," I replied. Gary's face cracked into a grin, and the other guys who were to accompany us on the hunt were quick to follow. What was all the fuss about? These little gray guys couldn't be that difficult to hit, could they?

"Pete Blakeley, pleased to meet you," I replied, sticking my hand out at the same time. The effect on the dogs was instant. They completely ignored everyone else and focused their attentions on me. Have you ever noticed how dogs always drift into a kind of speculative semi-nervous-verging-on-aggressive mode when they are confronted with something that appears different, smells different, and more important, sounds strange to them? Milo, who looked like a Labrador cross and was obviously the alpha dog, rumbled a low growl at the sound of the alien accent. The other members of the pack looked equally menacing, as though they were ready to back him up.

"They won't touch you, Bubba," Gary said, grinning reassuringly, as I was quickly surrounded by the slavering pack. The handshake was brief; I decided not to venture too close to the five sets of snapping jaws.

"You wanna see some doves?" Gary continued. Now, I must admit, that did seem like a good idea. During the 450 mile or so journey I had only spotted a grand total of three, and by now my genetically engineered cynicism had kicked in. I was hoping the journey had not been wasted.

We all loaded into two of the trucks and were soon bouncing along one of the dusty, red rusty tracks that bisected the landscape. Huge red dust clouds chased us along the farm tracks until the trucks slowed to a halt next to an old abandoned schoolhouse. The building was surrounded by the skeletal remains of what had once been a healthy stand of elm trees.

"Trees are a-dyin', no-one knows why," Gary told me.

As we climbed out of the trucks and the vehicle doors slammed, doves spilled from the surrounding trees with their characteristic whistling wing beats, not in ones and twos, but several dozen. More trees revealed even more doves. OK, so I was visibly impressed, and Gary's face was a picture of triumphant "I told you so." I looked forward to the morning.

Next morning, as the alarm sounded at 5 a.m. I was already wide awake. The noise galvanized me into action and I staggered out of bed, excitedly emptying the contents of my Wally's bag onto the floor. I pulled on my cammo pants and shirt, realizing immediately that size large here in Texas isn't remotely similar to large in Scotland.

I glanced at my reflection in the closet mirror and realized that I looked like a Japanese sniper out of the film *The Bridge on the River Kwai*. I hesitantly peered into the kitchen and breathed a sigh of relief as I saw that everyone was dressed the same.

Over a hasty and tasty breakfast of coffee and blueberry muffins, we planned our attack with military precision. Gary and the guys knew the area well and decided that an undisturbed strip of trees to the west should be the most productive. Four of the guys were placed at strategic intervals at one end, but Gary's son Dustin and I drew the short straws. We were nominated to walk the tree line and flush the birds.

As we worked our way down the tree line, I could see the doves zipping in and out of the foliage like fleas on a hedgehog's back. I knew that an eruption of birds as we came to the end of the tree line would be inevitable. I nervously flicked the safety forward in anticipation, just as the first ones began breaking cover and flying back over us. Take the first one out there with the choke barrel, the second one a bit nearer with the cylinder. That should do it. I lifted onto the first bird and touched the trigger.

Unfortunately, by the time the shot arrived at the place where the dove was, he suddenly wasn't. Next shot, same result. Two bangs, but no doves. To everyone's amusement, I missed them both cleanly. Of course, Gary didn't miss it.

"Hot damn, Limey!" Gary bellowed (just in case there was anyone out there within earshot who missed it) and then added with a chuckle, "They both flew right through the pattern! They'll do that to you!"

Before I could reload, the rest of the doves dispersed at a speed that would have made an Exocet missile envious. My confidence was dented, and I stopped to ponder for a moment. I've shot wily, heather-hugging driven grouse on some of the best moors in Scotland and stratospheric driven pheasants all over the UK. Compared to those, the doves looked relatively easy. But the fact was, I wasn't in Scotland. I was here in Texas shooting at things that just aren't where they're supposed to be when you pull the trigger.

What was even more surprising was that this was opening day. These birds had never been shot at before. The slightest detection of movement in their peripheral vision triggered immediate evasive action, and they rolled and pitched like skirmishing MiG fighters. Milo the dog looked at me in disgust.

But things got better. The next bird to run the gauntlet curled back and came past me well out into the field of millet. I kept the gun out of my shoulder to better develop his erratic line correctly, exaggerated the lead, and the split second the butt touched my shoulder, triggered the shot. I was relieved to see the bird crumple and plummet earthward. I marked the spot and walked over to pick him up. I examined the dove closely, because, until then, I had never had the opportunity. The dove looked smaller than it did in flight. The wing size was large in relation to the body size, and the wings were scimitar shaped, more or less similar to a falcon, which would account for the rapid acceleration. The pointed tail gave it the appearance of a pigeon/parakeet hybrid. Maybe the tail was the secret of the aerial agility of these guys? I thought for a moment. I have seen hen pheasants come off the side of a Scottish mountain with a 60-mile-an-hour gale behind them demonstrate similar maneuvers as they spot the waiting guns.

With pheasants, the secret is to keep the gun out of the shoulder until you trigger the shot and ignore the sideways deviation in the flight pattern, taking the bird well out in front with the choke barrel. This also seems to work with doves, but one thing I noticed as the day progressed was that I was overleading some of the birds. They could accelerate quickly, but because of the small size they just did not have the momentum of a bird with more body weight and would make heavy going of it when flying into a stiff headwind with a full cargo of sunflower seeds. With a strong tailwind the situation was reversed, and I needed to accelerate the gun well through them. Small birds with rapid wing beats give the illusion of speed; the reverse is true of large birds such as geese.

My first trip to Muleshoe was an eyeopener and I relied on Gary's expertise and information to get me into an opportune position. Since that first day, I have had the opportunity to do lots of dove hunting. Unfortunately, most of us don't do our homework before a dove hunting trip. There are certain things that we can do to make sure that we optimize our situation to guarantee a more productive hunt.

Reading the Field

First and foremost, we need to make sure we are familiar with our surroundings before we get there. As with many other migratory bird species, doves have predictable feeding patterns and will use the same locations until they decide the time has come to migrate. North American species are particularly susceptible to changes in temperature, which can be frustrating; a field that is scouted two days before can be totally devoid of doves after a sudden cold front moves through.

Reading the field is as important for the successful dove hunter as it is for the successful salmon fisherman who reads the purls on a salmon river. My fishing tackle and gunshop was on the Border Esk, one of the premier salmon and sea-trout rivers in Scotland. Every year visiting anglers, armed with the most expensive tackle that money could buy, would be frustrated by their efforts to catch fish. But the locals—familiar with every eddy, rock for-

mation, and oxygen-rich salmon lie—were always successful. The dove field is the same.

Doves leave their roosting areas early in the morning to feed. There are certain areas that doves find more attractive for an overnight roost, whether a stand of a few trees with sparse vegetation, a disused windmill, or a few power lines cutting across the field. Doves are creatures of habit; once you recognize these areas and make a note of them, setting up within range of them may be productive. Where are the birds coming from and going too, and why? Some areas will be obvious to the casual observer, but other areas may be less apparent, even to the most observant dove hunter. Often, careful scrutiny will reveal some productive feeding secrets.

Food may be abundant, but because of this, it may be difficult to home in on one area that is more productive than another and the birds will happily flit enticingly in multiple directions from one food source to another, often frustratingly just out of range. So sometimes, you may need a different strategy. Most birds that depend largely on a diet of seed require two basic things to help with their digestion. Water is one, and during the days these feeding forays will also be interspersed with the need to drink. It is well known that one of the most productive areas may be seated next to a pond (or tank in Texas) in the evening as the gray speedsters drop in for a sundowner.

Grit is the second essential digestion aid. Careful scrutiny can often reveal that many fields have an area where heavy rain runoff has exposed a sandy or gritty area that is attractive to the birds. During the day they will oscillate back and forth between the areas of food, water, and grit, and this is where some preseason scouting by the prudent hunter can pay handsome dividends. If at all possible, a roughly triangular flight path between an area of grit, water, and food will be ideal. When the birds are full, they will head into a patch of trees to rest for a while and then repeat the process often two or sometimes three times during the

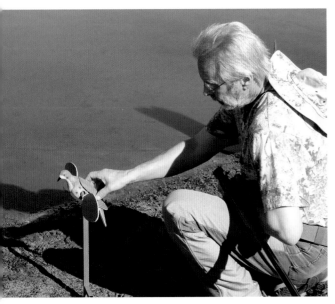

Setting your decoys near water can pay dividends. Here I am using a Mojo dove.

course of the day. Windy days may not be as productive; the birds seem to know that the amount of energy they need to expend to sally back and forth against a strong headwind may be too much.

Once an area is picked out, you need to set up a few decoys. I prefer the full body style with perhaps a Mojo dove or two with rotating wings. It's surprising how a flash of a wing in the morning light can turn a dove from a long way. As with waterfowl, doves are social birds, and just one or two doves coming in regularly to the decoys will attract more. In a treed area where doves are coming in, the decoys can be placed in some of the trees.

Gear

All the members of the *Columba* species are the wiliest and sharpest-eyed birds and turn quickly at the sight of a gun or the glint of the setting sun on a set of barrels. One year, as I was sitting with a client at a private ranch in the Texas panhandle, I watched approaching doves repeatedly turn as

they spotted something that disturbed them. Both the client and I were well camouflaged and positioned snugly in the margins of a field of millet, but the doves were turning long before they came within range. The problem, I discovered, was the female client's rather large diamond earrings and sparkly Rolex! The lady looked perplexed as I politely asked her to remove them. She was understandably reluctant, but it did the trick; the doves flew much more obligingly as a result.

Camouflage, or at least muted clothing early on in the season, is necessary. Later in the season when the birds have been shot at a few times, full camouflage is best. You will do a lot of walking, so a pair of lightweight, comfortable shoes is a must, as is a pair of plastic lens safety glasses. I have had

This woman's camouflaged clothing is excellent, but there is a problem. Doves have excellent eyesight. Sparkly jewelry like hers will turn doves from 100 yards away.

many conversations with shooters who have been shot during hectic activity on the dove field. Most of the time this is a stray pellet from a shooter discharging a shot in an errant direction and will be no more than a painful sting on the arm or leg. But if the same pellet hits you in the eye, you may be blinded. Eyesight is precious, and I never hunt without eye protection. A seat or stool is essential too, and I usually use the simple, lightweight folding camo variety.

Another type of stool is the swivel-topped Evans Sports bucket, which works well. When you are sitting on the swivel seat, you can easily reposition for doves coming from a different direction because the top turns 360 degrees. If you prefer to take your shots from a seated position, one of these stools can be a godsend. Once you get used to the swiveling action, this has the advantage of allowing you to keep your shoulders level as you develop the line of each bird. Failure to do this may encourage you to drop off line, and the muzzles of the gun will prescribe an arc as you run out of swing. The bucket also has a cooler and a container to transport your harvested doves, ammo, and decoys.

Regardless of the type of seat you favor, you need to learn to sit still for long periods in between the activity. The birds will quickly spot movement and will respond by dipping and diving to take evasive action. The guy who stretches his legs, practices his gun mount and swing, and fidgets all the time will spook birds so fast that they will flare well before they come into range.

Some hunters shoot from the seat, and others may be tempted to stand up and shoot from an upright position. With doves, the four beat shooting rhythm described in chapter 7 works well, and in fact will increase your success rate many times, probably more on doves than any other bird.

A dog is essential for dove hunting, especially for hunting mourning doves out on the plains where the harvest has been close-cropped. The gray and brown coloration and the creamy breast

The Evans Sport bucket is a well-thought-out accessory for the dove hunting enthusiast. The bucket contains a cooler and shell pouches and the top swivels to allow you to develop the line of the birds more easily from a sitting position.

feathers of the birds blend perfectly with the leaves and corn stubble as soon as they hit the ground. It sometimes pays, when shooting over this type of terrain, to let the well-trained dog retrieve while you keep shooting. A successful and productive shoot, especially in the southern plains with often high temperatures, can be hard on a dog, some-

A good dog is essential on a dove hunt.

times fatal if heat stroke kicks in. Always have a supply of cold water on hand, and never become too engrossed in the action to ignore the dog's needs; stop shooting if necessary, and if at all possible, stop occasionally to let the dog have a swim.

I like an over-and-under for doves, and mine is a 30-inch barreled Browning Citori 20-gauge sporting. The gun is slightly heavier than the regular field model, and I find that with this slight increase in weight the overall handling dynamics are better. I use 1-ounce shells with 7 1/2 shot.

After my first shoot all those years ago in Muleshoe, we drank American beer and dined on jalapeño-stuffed dove breasts and deer sausage from the barbeque. There was lots of jovial bullwhip with congenial folks under the clear Texas sky with a million stars and a perfect moon.

"Well, Limey, how'd you do?" Gary asked, grinning widely. He already, I suspect, knew the answer. I wasn't bragging; in fact nobody was. Those little gray guys had me dancing on my toes. I hit the ones that I expected to miss, and sometimes I missed the ones that I expected to hit. Some of them left me feeling that I couldn't hit a cow on the arse with a banjo. But I loved every minute of it.

CHAPTER 11

Pheasants, Grouse, and Partridges

The Stately homes of England, how beautiful they stand,
To prove the upper classes, still have the upper hand.

—*Noel Coward*

Today in the US, the gaudy pheasant is everyone's favorite. It's a big, handsome bird that always shows up in winter scenes on Christmas cards and on birthday cards for shooting sportsmen. Most hunters think the ringneck is a native species and are surprised to learn that they were in fact introduced here in 1881. On March 13 of that year, fifty or so Chinese ringnecks arrived in Port Townsend on the ship Otago, together with other Chinese birds and plants. The United States consul, Owen Nickerson Denny, and his wife, Gertrude Jane Hall Denny, shipped them over from Shanghai, hoping to establish a breeding population in their home state of Oregon. Sadly, many of the pheasants succumbed to the rigors of the long and arduous journey. The remaining survivors were released in an area of the lower Columbia River, but it could not be confirmed if these birds actually survived.

More birds were shipped in 1882 and 1884 to the Willamette Valley, and this time a successful breeding population was established. The colorful game birds proved to be prolific breeders and also welcome fare for the table. The population quickly spread throughout Oregon and the northern states.

Push-and-Block

Here in the United States, the mention of a pheasant hunt conjures up a scene of frantic flushing dogs and hunters walking waist deep through swaying Kansas cornfields. In the UK, we would class this as walked up shooting. In the United States, I was told it was called push-and-block hunting. The line of guns (pushers) and dogs walked the field and drove the birds toward the blockers who waited at the end of the field.

I knew from my exploits in Scotland that pheasants didn't like to fly and preferred to run ahead of the dogs with the stamina of a marathon runner. Late-season wily old birds take this to the extreme. When beating at Westerhall Estate, I have on several occasions seen a large cock bird scuttle in front of my dog just out of reach, until he finally became airborne, cackling loudly but by now, just out of shot!

When hunting pheasants this way, it is always best to try to walk into the wind. The reason for this is threefold. Pheasants, especially late-season pheasants that have been shot at a few times, are smart. Noise carries a long way with the wind, and the noise of a vehicle engine and the slam of a truck door will have them sprinting for cover. At Westerhall Estate in Scotland where I was both a beater and a gun on select keeper's days, there was sometimes no choice. Some of the approach roads would wind upward, following the contours of the hills. The pheasants could hear the drone of the Land Rover engines from well over a mile away, and we could often see the birds sprinting for cover as the vehicles approached. If you can, approach into the wind to minimize this.

Tatton Hall, the neoclassical mansion at Tatton Park, Cheshire, is one of England's finest historical estates. In 1795, the estate covered 251,000 acres. Today it is owned and operated by the National Trust and is open to the public. GEORGE LITTLER AND PETER SPOONER, TATTON PARK PHOTO

The second reason to walk into the wind is that pheasants are big birds relative to the size of their wings. A hen pheasant will fly faster and lift quicker than a rooster. That may not be that important here in the US where, on wild birds, there is a rooster-only rule. A big rooster pheasant will become airborne much quicker as he catapults himself upward and feels the wind beneath his pinions—this will allow him to lift and flare away quickly.

The third reason is that the dogs will be able to smell the birds much better and home in on them by following the scent trail of the birds, carried toward them on the wings of the wind. Depending on the day, some of the wily old birds will still inevitably slip past the dogs. When they eventually run out of cover, these birds will hunker down, relying on their camouflage, and they will still hold tight until you almost step on them. Then they noisily and unexpectedly explode from cover, nearly giving you a heart attack!

Push-and-block hunts require a lot of walking. They aren't for the frail of limb and short of breath. The pushers must move slowly and keep in line with each other. This is important; pheasants that are moving in front of the line will hunker down to listen to the approach of the walking guns. A pusher who walks too fast will create a gap that birds can slip through. When covering a large area, if you have a shortage of pushers, a coordinated zigzag across the field may get good results. Stop occasionally. Pheasants, especially late-season birds that have been shot at, will be nervous. An occasional pause will often make these birds lift.

The first time I experienced a push-and-block hunt, I was a guest at a private ranch in the flint hills of northern Kansas. Over dinner that night I asked my host why they didn't use a sewlin line to encourage the birds to become airborne, instead of the blockers.

"In Scotland," I informed my hosts, "we use a sewlin line to turn the birds." At that time I thought that maybe American pheasant hunters employed something similar, but it might have been given a different name. But during the

A driven pheasant hunt in progress in Scotland. The sewlin line is used to turn the birds.

course of the conversation, it became clear that nobody had ever used or heard of anything like it before. So for anyone who is interested, here is a detailed description of the sewlin line.

The line is made by tying 1 1/2-inch white strips of plastic fertilizer bags onto baler twine, the strong polypropylene string that ranchers use. These strips are tied on at approximate 1-yard intervals, and the complete sewlin line is then wound onto a cable drum. To use the line, which could be over 100 yards long, one end of it is tied to a fence post or something similar at the end of a field and a brush shank is then inserted through the cable drum. The line operator then runs the line out across the end of the field. As the birds approach, the operator jiggles the line so that the white plastic strips move. The pheasants will not, under any circumstances, cross the line and will flush and become airborne as soon as they see it.

The sewlin line isn't a new idea, and we have used it in Scotland for years. Interestingly, a similar ploy was used on tiger hunts in India. At the turn of the century, tiger hunting from elephants was a favorite pastime of the maharajas. They would pursue the tigers through the jungles on several of these elephants, and each giant pachyderm would carry on its back a mobile shooting platform so that the maharajah could shoot from relative safety. Beaters were also employed to flush the tigers from the undergrowth, and to prevent the tigers from turning back, a similar sewlin line would be used. In this case, a skein of white silk cloth would be run out across the jungle by a coolie, and believe it or not, this was enough to turn a tiger so that the maharaja could get the chance of a shot. This may sound incredible, but I assure you, this was the way they would do it!

After my first push-and-block hunt in Kansas, and subsequent hunts in Nebraska and South Dakota, I found out that a sewlin line or anything like it is not permitted in the States.

Narrow-Angle Shots

Hunting over dogs like this will mean that the majority of the shots will be narrow-angle shots requiring minimum lead. As the bird gets further away, many shooters make the mistake of thinking that he will require more lead as the range increases. It's easy to see why. A big rooster jumps out of the corn field almost under your feet and

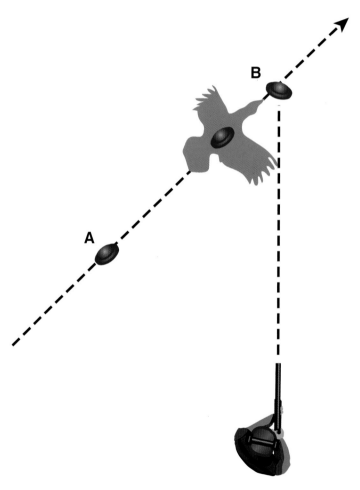

As the bird gets farther away, moving from A to B, the angle relative to your shooting position is decreasing. The perceived lead is less as a result.

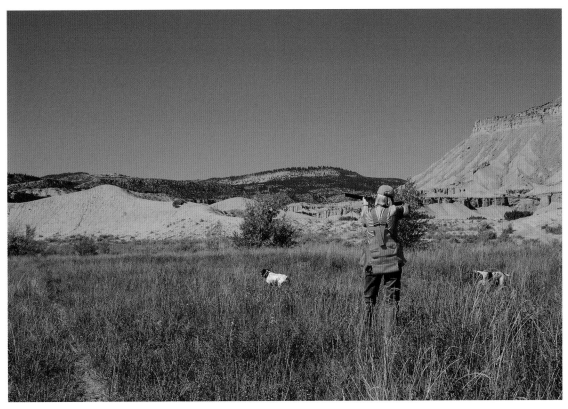

Most push-and-block birds will be flying directly away from you. CASTLE VALLEY OUTDOORS PHOTO

rattles almost straight away from you, at a slight angle to your position, gathering speed quickly. This is one of the few times that you miss in front with this shot.

As the range increases, you would assume the pattern would need to placed further in front of the bird for successful interception. However, in reality, increased perceived lead (the amount the shooter thinks he needs) on this type of shot isn't necessary. If the rooster angles away to the left or right, increasing his relative angle to your shooting position more, he will need more lead. But if he gets further away and still maintains a narrow angle relative to your shooting position, he won't. As he flies, the angle between you and the bird is closing. The angle of the bird dictates the perceived lead requirement. The unit lead section explains this in detail.

Good dogs are essential. As pheasants are flushed in this way, most times they will be flying directly away from you or, at least initially, at a slight angle to your shooting position. This makes them less vulnerable to your shot pattern because they are shielding their heads and necks. Wounded birds are, unfortunately, sometimes inevitable, and a good dog will find these birds so they can be dispatched as quickly as possible.

Birds are killed by a pellet or pellets that find their way to a vital organ, and pheasants are big birds. Some shooters use a 20 gauge, and although this would be acceptable in many cases, in my opinion, the nature of push-and-block shooting requires a 12 gauge. Wounded birds that don't receive a lethal dose of pellets immediately will hit the ground running and often find their way into

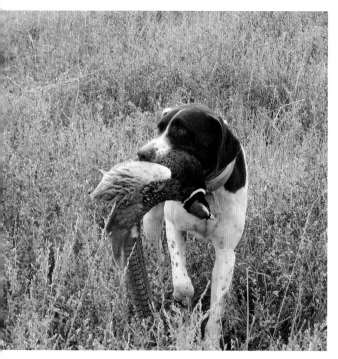

A textbook retrieve. CASTLE VALLEY OUTDOORS PHOTO

thick cover to die later from either loss of blood or asphyxia from a lung shot. I feel it is always best to overgun than undergun; we owe it to the birds.

Driven Pheasant Hunts

The other method of pheasant hunting, which is growing in popularity here in the US, is the driven pheasant hunt. When I first moved here in 1997, the members at both Westside Sporting Grounds in Houston and the Dallas Gun Club would listen wide-eyed and open-mouthed when I would tell them stories of driven pheasant shoots in Scotland. At that time, driven pheasant shoots were almost unheard of over here. I was surprised. Today, here in the States, quality driven pheasant shoots are available in several locations. America has the terrain and temperature, and American sportsmen have the temperament to enjoy this style of European shooting.

In driven shooting, birds are flushed from cover by beaters in such a way that they fly over the prestationed, waiting guns. These stations where the shooters are positioned are called pegs. Driven pheasant and partridge shooting have a very similar format, but the terrain and topography of both have a few differences. Years ago, the grey partridge was the main game bird for the Victorian and Edwardian sportsmen. In those days, farming was simple; arable farms were small, patchwork quilts of crisscrossed hedges, ditches, and drains. Today, as farming has become more commercial and efficiently mechanized, the hedgerows have been ripped out to provide larger, more commercially viable areas and larger fields. Unfortunately, the mixed arable land that is essential grey partridge habitat is gone forever. Whereas the pheasant is at home in more mountainous, heavily treed regions, the partridge favors mixed farmland with rolling hills and tall hedgerows similar to the topography of much of the land in the south of England. Neither the pheasant nor the partridge are suited to the moorland areas favored by their cousin, the red grouse. Red grouse are shot over open, barren moorland with the guns and loaders standing in grouse butts (similar to hides or blinds), which run in lines across the hills.

This style of pheasant hunting originated in England, in East Anglia, around 1875. For the privileged few, these organized driven pheasant shoots, where beaters would tap their way through the woodlands of the great sporting estates and flush hundreds of birds over the waiting guns, became a way of life. King Edward VII, at that time the Prince of Wales, was dedicated to the sport, and there is little doubt that he was instrumental in turning the shoots into social occasions. The organization of these Victorian and Edwardian shoots was formidable; they developed into social extravaganzas on an alarming scale. Transport for the guest guns and the beaters needed to be well organized, in addition to lunch and food arrangements, payment of staff, and last but not least, something that is always a worry in the UK, the possibility of inclement weather.

The keepers at these shoots were responsible for rearing the birds from the egg right up until the time when the six-week-old poults were released, first into flight pens and eventually liberated into the wild. The flight pen was a large area of ground, often several hundred feet in diameter, surrounded with wire mesh, usually with a water source running through it. A hot wire installed around the perimeter kept the vermin out, and funnels around the outside guided the young birds back into the safety of the pen during the overnight hours.

On the day of the shoot, the keepers were expected to know precisely (depending on weather conditions and wind direction) where the birds would fly and position the guns accordingly. If the big shoot days were successful and the keeper could put on a good show of testing birds over the guns, he would be rewarded well at the end of the season.

Today the preparation for these elaborate events is just as complex. The dedicated shoot host anticipates a long-term relationship with his clientele and, ultimately, the repeat business that the enjoyment of his paying guests will bring in the future.

I feel very privileged to say that I have shot driven pheasants on some of the best estates in Scotland, including the Duke of Buccleuch's estate in Langholm, where I owned and operated my fishing tackle and gun shop, Border Tackle and Guns.

The Earl of Dalkeith's grouse moors surrounding Langholm were at one time considered to be one of the best in the world. The Scottish record red grouse bag stands at 1,261½ brace off the Roan Fell, on August 30, 1911. Sadly today the big bags of yesteryear have gone, but not forever, I hope. I have walked the purple heather-clad grouse moors surrounding Langholm with my Labrador retrievers many times. Until recently, the historic Langholm moors made a significant economic contribution to an area that hitherto was

incapable of supporting little else, apart from the sheep and wilds goats that still inhabit the area.

Recently there has been a dramatic increase (despite the downturn in the present economy) in traveling to the UK for such a hunt. The reason? I firmly believe that the Brits do a better job of the tightly organized and well-planned driven shoot day than anyone else in the shooting world. I believe also that most of the visiting guns are enthralled when they savor the unique experience of our ancient estates and magnificent country houses, each steeped in a colorful history. Add to this all the pomp and ceremony that's thrown in, and you have an attraction that would be hard to beat anywhere. If you have decided to journey across the pond for your first driven pheasant hunt, here are some of the finer points of the game.

Your host will probably arrange to meet you at the airport and transport you to your accommodation, usually a historic country house or, in some cases on the top quality shoots, a castle. The evening dinner on the night before the shoot will probably involve some serious wining and dining, especially if you are shooting driven birds in Scotland. Tread carefully here! One double malt too many the night before, followed by a full cholesterol breakfast in the morning is not the best recipe for straight shooting! A day's driven pheasant is expensive; a serious day's gun swinging may be spoiled with the added burden of a queasy stomach.

The next day, if you are lucky, will be a calm morning with light wind and no rain in the forecast. The birds won't fly well if it's raining too hard. The low winter sun splashes everything with amber and gold, and the hoar frost sparkles the moisture drops on the bracken with myriad colors, like a quality crystal wineglass. It looks almost idyllic, with a flavor of soft surrealism.

On the first drive—and there may be six drives during the day—you will be asked to pick a peg number by the keeper. These are numbered ivory pegs, and they will usually be selected from a leather wallet. The number you select is the place you will take on the first drive. On subsequent drives you will move up two places each time, but listen carefully because some shoots move up three. Try not to forget your peg number.

The estate vehicles will drop you off as near to your peg as possible, but there may still be a long walk ahead of you, burdened with gun, kit, and cartridges. The keeper signals the way, nodding you toward the steeply descending path that winds down a wooded slope. Timber posts have been knocked in at intervals down the side to assist your descent. As you reach the bottom, you discover that the muddy, downward track you tread eventually levels out. The pathway continues, following the melodic meanderings of a small, boulder-strewn river.

By now, that thing of beauty that all the guys were drooling over last night in the lounge bar, with the French walnut stock that glows like the cape of a November cock and the exquisitely carved fences, feels as heavy as a sack of Irish potatoes. As you reach your peg, blowing out steam in the icy air like an old locomotive, you realize that you're at the bottom of a steep gorge. In front of you is a high wooded escarpment and behind you another one.

Your neighboring gun politely squeezes past you on the narrow track as he walks to his peg 30 yards to your right. You look back up the pathway, and you can see another gun making his way to his peg on the left. Out of courtesy and before the shooting starts, you acknowledge that you are aware of the position of your neighboring guns by either a wave of the hand or hat.

You open your shooting stick and settle down on it, grateful for the brief respite, but then you remember why you are there. You need to get ready for the onslaught of birds. The new gun smells faintly of gun oil and exudes elegance as you free it from its slip. Better have a few energetic slashes with it at imaginary birds, you think. You diligently practiced your gun-mounting technique

for weeks, and it feels as though it has paid off handsomely. You are pleased with yourself, smugly satisfied as the gun comes repeatedly into your shoulder pocket with unerring accuracy. That should do, you think. Now there's just enough time for a quick breather as the beaters line out.

So what exactly is a beater? On the large estates in Scotland on all driven shoots, the birds are pushed out over the waiting guns using beaters, local guys who work for the love of the game. They are usually self-professed experts on such interesting topics as fishing, fighting, ferreting, consuming alcoholic beverages, and the anatomy of pretty ladies. These guys are the backbone of the shoot, and the success of the drive and the hard work of the gamekeeper ultimately depend on a good supply of knowledgeable beaters. They form a long line up at the edge of the woods or fields and tap their way through it with hazel sticks, braving the tangle of undergrowth, inclement weather, hangovers, unruly livestock, and low shooting guns, to flush the birds.

One of these guys will have a clicker, which he will press every time he hears a shot so that the keeper knows exactly how many shots have been fired on each drive. Often the beaters will walk 10 to 15 miles during the day over difficult terrain; in fact they will do anything to ensure the success of your day and all for the princely sum of about $40. And you thought the days of the feudal system, peasantry, and serfdom were over? Apparently not. Luckily for the shoot organizers, the money isn't the attraction for any of these guys. At the end of the season, the estate holds a keeper's day where the beaters are invited to shoot for free. I've done it hundreds of times for over the last twenty years and thoroughly enjoy it.

There will be twenty to thirty or so beaters in a line on each drive to keep the birds moving in front of this line at a steady pace. Some of the beaters will have dogs, and these dogs must be under control to ensure the success of the drive. An unruly dog that rushes forward and scatters the birds

Beaters on a driven pheasant shoot. BLIXT & CO. PHOTO

will be a severe detriment to a successful drive. The keeper knows his job perfectly and will orchestrate the shoot with a two-way radio. The idea is to hold the birds together as cohesively as possible until the flushing point is reached, which is usually at the top of the hill. The birds—there could be as many as a couple thousand in one drive—will be forced out of the thick cover and over the waiting guns a few at a time, not all at once. On a good day you can expect at least five drives per day, depending on the quota of birds to be shot.

Keeper and beaters push forward in unison, methodically tapping their way, poking the birds out of their hiding places in the cover with their hazel sticks. "Look for 'em, lads," the head keeper orders. The birds are sitting tight and reluctant to fly. Who can blame them? Pheasants are smart. Some of the

wily old cocks let the beating line pass and then try to break back, but they are spotted by a flanker and turned. Flankers are simply older beaters, usually past their sell-by date and less energetic than the younger guys. Flankers are positioned at strategic points to stop the birds from breaking out and flying the wrong way. Each will be equipped with a hazel stick like the rest of the beaters, but theirs has a white plastic fertilizer bag nailed to it so that it can be used as a flag. When the birds, which are about to fly in the wrong direction, are spotted, the flanker waves the flag rapidly. The noise of the flapping flag and the flash of white turns them.

An eerie silence precedes the action. In the deep wooded valley where you stand, very little sun penetrates the tangle of trees. The temperature has dropped below freezing, and as you stand motionless, icy cold fingers of the early morning air begin to penetrate your warm clothing. Each breath you take whisps away, drifting ghostlike across the cascading silver stream. You hear distant noise, faint, hollow tapping and the rustle of dogs crashing through the tangle of undergrowth, but still a long way off.

"Hold the line lads," you can just make out, as someone's young, unruly springer spaniel runs ahead.

The air is highly charged with anticipation. Suddenly you can see the beaters. They are systematically working their way through a thin line of spruce plantation on the side of a hill and heading toward the main tree line of majestic, mighty oaks.

Your pulse rate quickens, and your ears strain for more audible clues. You hear the metallic, cockling call of the first rooster to break cover. He's been spotted by a more experienced dog, deep in the heart of the dark, recessed cover under a fallen oak. As he realizes his cover is blown, he quickly extricates himself from the seemingly impossible tangle of bracken and briars and catapults his heavy body upward on his powerful legs, just escaping the snap of the springer spaniel hot on his heels. His straining pinions lift him skyward through the latticework of the spruce branches, and the sudden sense of freedom spurs him on.

He's yours, you think! But as you lift the gun in anticipation, he quickly gathers the wind beneath his wings and, as he rises above the canopy of the mighty oaks, curls out of sight before you can get on him.

The distant pop of a gun tells you that someone farther down the line has had a crack at him. Other birds appear quickly, some so high that they are indistinct and nebulous as they sail over the tangled tops of the spruces into the swirling mist of the perfect Scottish morning.

Soon the sky seems full, a tapestry of flushing birds. You almost panic, wondering which one to take. It is easy to become mesmerized with so many birds. The words of your shooting coach

ring in your ears. He has taught you well: "Look through the bouquet, pick your bird, and develop his line." Ah, yes, now you remember.

Don't put the gun in your shoulder too early. Remember that the easiest way to develop the line of any tall pheasant is with a combination of arms and body movement. The shots should be triggered ideally just as the butt of the gun comes snugly into your shoulder.

Remember also that the perception of lead on the bird that is farther out is less than when he is directly overhead. If possible, take the first bird out in front on the right with your choke barrel and the next one slightly on the left with your open choke. It's called a right and left, and it works well for the right-shouldered shooter and keeps the gun tucked into your face. Take the left bird first and you will find that you will push the gun away from your face. The left-shouldered gun should take the left-hand bird first. You need a smooth progressive swing as you get onto the first bird. Don't switch from one bird to another, and don't look for the second bird of your right and left until you have killed the first bird.

Have the courage to trigger your shots as you come onto the line of the birds, and they'll fold as quickly as a bad poker hand. Unfortunately that hasn't happened on your first shot. The spent shells spew out with a hollow pop as you open the gun. Your gloved but cold fingers fumble in the pouch for two more shells, and you curse quietly as one of them misses the chamber and falls into the hoar-frosted grass at your feet. You reach down to retrieve it and hurriedly give it a quick wipe on your sleeve before dropping it into the chamber. The gun closes with a satisfying clunk and you're ready to try again.

You peer upward, and the air above you is filled with a melee of birds; there's plenty more to have a go at. You pick out a handsome, high-flying cock and blot him out with your barrels. He's in the bag, you think. You give him both barrels in quick succession, but he never falters.

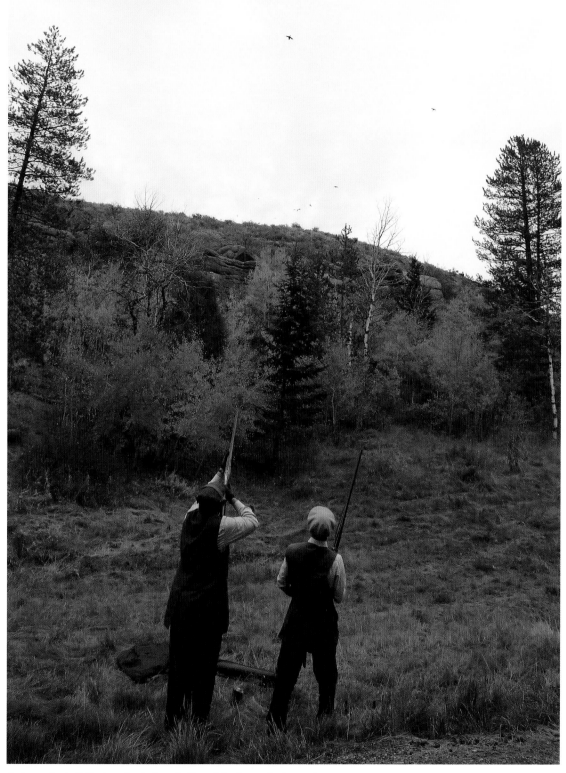

Archangels, indistinct and nebulous in the mist of a perfect morning. BLIXT & CO. PHOTO

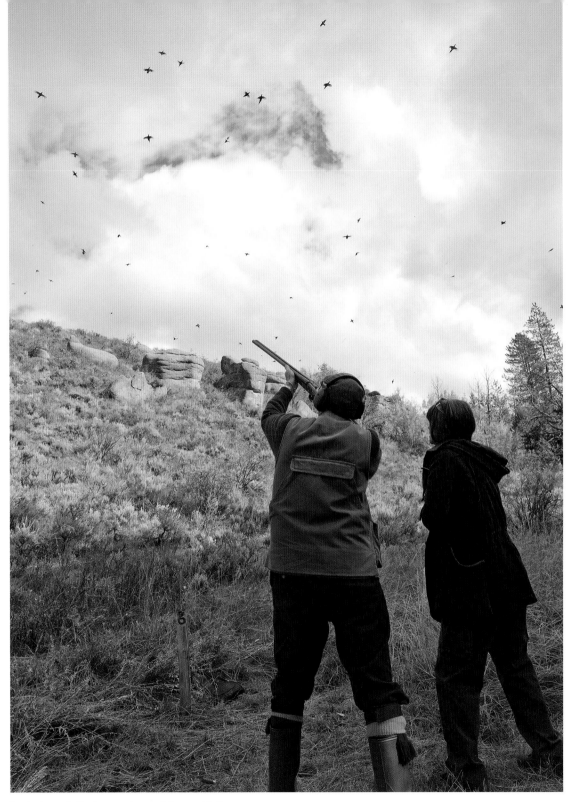

Look through the bouquet and pick your bird. BLIXT & CO. PHOTO

For twenty minutes or so (it seems like a lot longer), the action is fast and furious, and then the whistle blows, signaling that the drive is over.

Whatever happens, don't shoot after the whistle, however tempting it may seem as that one last cock rattles over, taunting all the guns. You almost breathe a sigh of relief. You're hot now, as if you've had a grueling workout at the gym. You have time to reflect, to compose yourself before the next drive. You look down in disbelief at the pile of spent hulls round your feet. Did you really fire all those shots for just three birds? I'm afraid so, but it's early yet, and there's another five drives to go. A quick swig of peach brandy from your hip flask consoles your bruised ego.

With your enthusiasm revived now, it's off to the next drive. As the day progresses, you redeem yourself. You begin to realize that developing the line correctly, not lead, is the most important thing. You learn at last how to push through and not rush through, and you manage to connect with more birds as a result.

At the end of each drive, Labradors and springer spaniels, spurred on by their handlers, flit like field mice through the undergrowth and mop the birds up between drives.

"Where is it? Seek 'em out then!" the dog handlers enthusiastically encourage their charges. The dogs, mud splattered, tongues lolling happily and with their rudders quivering like tuning forks with excitement, are a pleasure to behold. At the end of the day, the dogs (and their handlers) will be exhausted. These are all hand-picked dogs. Only the best are good enough, and they know their job and do it well.

Moving in tandem with the dogs and handlers, the game cart is filling up nicely, gathering the harvested birds from the stockpiles at the edge of the rides. Some of the more experienced dogs and handlers will be positioned a long way to the rear of the line of guns, often up to half a mile, because a really tall pheasant, coming down from forty yards or more, may have received a lethal dose of

pellets, but he may still set his wings and glide a long way.

Etiquette plays a big part in all driven shoots, not just for politeness, but for safety reasons. As you look to the front, try to imagine a line straight ahead. All the birds that come over you 45 degrees the left and right of this line, and to the front and rear, are legitimate birds. (See illustration on page 7.) In other words, you have a 90-degree arc of fire in front of you and the same behind.

With driven pheasant and partridge, don't take low birds below the tree line and don't fire a shot after the whistle or other signal of the end of the drive. The keeper and beaters know their job perfectly, and for the next few minutes there will be a

Reaching for a tall bird. BLIXT & CO. PHOTO

steady stream of birds coming over. Right-shoul-dered shooters should try to take a right bird first and then swing smoothly onto a left. Do it the opposite way and you will push the gun away from your face and lose the line. On these high birds, line is more important than lead. Take one bird out in front with your choke barrel and the next one directly above where he is most vulnerable.

There's more time than you think. Be patient and avoid the temptation of putting the gun in your shoulder too early; it's a mistake. The longer the gun's in your shoulder, the more conscious you will become of it. Don't commit to making the shot until you can carry it through in one smooth, assertive swing. Anything that looks as though it will fly better for one of your neighboring guns should be left for them, unless of course your neighbor is a good friend and you attempt to wipe his eye. This is when you shoot a bird, which is obviously not yours, just as your neighbor tries to get on it. Eye wiping is "not exactly cricket, old boy"—great fun but rude, and lots of guns do it.

Mr. Pheasant

I have one final story to tell you about pheasants. My house in Scotland was in the scenic valley of Bentpath, about a mile from Westerhall Estate and some of the best driven pheasants in the world. The release pens for Westerhall were in the Sitka spruce conifer plantations at the back of my property. As the birds became mature and ventured farther from the sanctuary of their release pen, I could look out the window in the mornings and see twenty pheasants or more scratching for food in my garden, almost like domestic chickens. One of these was an old English blackneck, a magnificent cock bird that stood out from the crowd and was far bigger than the rest. An old English blackneck doesn't have the white ring that other pheasants have. Instead these birds have a dark metallic, blue-green plumage on their heads and necks. They are easily recognizable and quite unique.

At the time, my daughter Hollie was three years old, and she soon learned to recognize this particular pheasant and christened him simply "Mr. Pheasant." This bird was smart; every time there was a shoot at Westerhall, as soon as the Land Rovers and estate vehicles carrying the beaters arrived, he would secrete himself in the shrubbery at the bottom of our garden. After the shoot, we always feared the worst, but miraculously, Mr. Pheasant would always escape the guns unscathed.

Each spring after the shooting season had ended, we would see him strutting his stuff on our lawn with a harem of hen pheasants, much to the amusement of our daughter Hollie. Some of these hen pheasants would actually nest in our garden, and over a three-year period, Mr. Pheasant became quite a celebrity. He would fly up to the kitchen window ledge and tap on it until my wife would respond, rewarding him with a handful of kitchen scraps. With this added bonus of gourmet food, he eventually became huge and defended his territory against all challengers. He was the Mike Tyson of the pheasant world.

One winter, after a particularly bleak period of gales, driving rain, snow, and freezing night temperatures, Mr. Pheasant was conspicuous by his absence. We no longer heard his early morning tattoo tapping on the kitchen window as he routinely begged for his breakfast. My daughter Hollie, who was now five, noticed this, and we feared the worst. Perhaps he had been off his guard one day and strayed too far from the sanctuary of our garden as a shoot at Westerhall was in progress.

A week went by and still no sign of Mr. Pheasant. We had almost given up hope of ever seeing him again. Then one cold and cloudy Sunday at lunchtime Hollie excitedly cried out as she spotted him underneath the kitchen window.

At first we thought she was mistaken; the pheasant outside the kitchen bore no resemblance to the one we had grown familiar with. But there was no mistaking the unique coloration of his metallic green cape; this was indeed Mr. Pheasant. No longer was he the splendid example he once was. He was in poor shape, thin, bedraggled, and soaking wet. He also had a pronounced cough and a limp. I suspected that he had pneumonia and didn't have much hope for him.

His favorite treats were peanuts, and my wife Alison threw a handful out of the window, but he ignored the lot. We tried crushed wheatmeal biscuits, another favorite, and still no response.

"How about some raisins?" I suggested. Raisins were Mr. Pheasant's all-time favorite, but they were also expensive, so he only very occasionally got some, usually if Alison had been baking.

"We don't have any," Alison replied. "I'm steeping them for the Christmas cake."

It was traditional in Scotland for families to bake their own Christmas cake. Alison loved to do it and always baked several, one for her mother and one each for her two aunts. Before the ingredients for the cake were mixed, it was a routine to soak the dried fruit, currants, sultanas, and raisins in either brandy or whisky.

Sure enough, a look in the pantry revealed that there was a large bowl filled with raisins steeping in a mixture of brandy and whisky. I threw a few out to the pheasant and watched his reaction. At first he ignored them, but then he gingerly swallowed a couple. Two hours later he was back for more and this time swallowed about ten or so.

I didn't expect the bird to make it through the night, but the next morning we were woken up early by an excited Hollie. Mr. Pheasant was once again outside the kitchen window. Hollie fed him some peanuts, and I (much to Alison's annoyance) fed him some more whisky-soaked raisins.

At the end of the week, Mr. Pheasant was strutting his stuff again, bolder than ever and completely recovered from his ordeal, much to the delight of Hollie. It's a true (and I like to think delightful) story. The whisky, there was no doubt in my mind, was the answer. After all, they don't call it the water of life in Scotland for nothing, do they?

Driven Grouse

Driven partridge shoots follow a similar format, but driven grouse is slightly different. The red grouse is to many the king of all game birds. In my opinion (and also that of many others), it is rightly prized as the crème de la crème of all game bird shooting. Driven red grouse shooting in the UK (and especially Scotland), believe it or not, is even more expensive than driven pheasant and partridge. First, the species is found nowhere else in the world. Second, it is impossible to rear the red grouse like other game birds. Grouse fly like no other bird. The bird has a strong, fast flight—faster even than the peregrine falcon in level flight. Red grouse fly in packs of twenty or more, hugging the contours of the moor like a Harrier jump jet, lifting at the last minute to skim over the grouse butts with an audible *whoosh* of their powerful pinions. I have heard the sound many times, and it is quite awe inspiring.

I have no doubt that some shoot organizers over here in the US almost sadistically rub their hands with glee and chuckle silently as their wallets swell as yet another unsuspecting American bird hunter books a couple of days' driven grouse shooting in Scotland. Like unwary lambs to the slaughter, they board their chosen aircraft and wing their way over the mighty Atlantic, full of expectation, knowing not what is to confront them as they land.

Because of the costs involved and the quality of the shotgunning required to hit them with any consistency, driven grouse shooting is not for the faint of heart. A days' driven grouse shooting on a Scottish moor is something that you will savor forever, possibly the absolute zenith of the shooting man's career. That said, in all honesty, it is best left for the experts in the shooting world . . . and also the ones with the most formidable wallets! For anyone who is thinking about taking the plunge, here is an account of what to expect.

Smaller than his cousin the pheasant, the red grouse is a tough bird. All grouse moors are wild, desolate places. The areas he inhabits are the windswept mountainous regions of northern England and Scotland. The red grouse is a deep reddish brown color speckled with white and chocolate. His legs and feet are not scaled like other birds, but heavily clad with coarse white feathers. The plumage is extra thick to give him insulation from the cold. It has to be—these areas are constantly buffeted by driving rain, snow, and merciless winds that are fierce enough to cut the face off a sheep. As a result, the grouse is a strong and agile flyer.

Access to the moor proper is difficult; short wheelbase Land Rovers or Suzuki Samurais and Argocats are the choice vehicles for scrambling up and down the positively precipitous narrow tracks. The progress of the vehicles is painfully slow. With complaining and patiently enduring engines and grinding gear boxes, they labor upward on the makeshift rock-strewn, rain-furrowed roads. Treacherous rocky skrees interspersed with tufts of tenacious purple heather appear at every turn. Boulders, standing precariously like ancient monoliths at the sides of the road, threaten to relinquish their hold from the sucking black peat and block your path.

A typical grouse moor. Believe it or not, there are forty-five grouse in this picture. The birds are approaching the butts, and because their coloration matches the backdrop of vegetation, as they contour the ground, they are very difficult to see. THOMAS KIER PHOTO

Eventually the zigzag journey ceases, and the vehicles grind gratefully to a halt on the top of the incline. The keepers, dogs, and gun handlers burst busily out of the vehicles. The dogs, mainly Labradors, explode from their kennel confines, all deep-chested dogs, with rudders quivering like tuning forks from the excitement. They know the game; their nervous systems are on overload as their handlers try to restrain their over-exuberant and wild-eyed charges.

Primitive pathways formed over centuries by countless sheep dissect the landscape, but beware, the area is interspersed with patches of treacherous peat bog that will suck a heavy Land Rover under. So its Shank's pony, I'm afraid—the first butts are another two miles or so of remorselessly walking ever upward through the purple heather for another thousand feet or so.

For the uninitiated, heather is a small, incredibly tough, wiry shrub, which grows to a maximum height of about 2 to 3 feet. Walking any distance through it is a nightmare. The keepers and beaters of yesteryear wore the traditional kilt when walking in the moors. The very thought brings tears to my eyes, and not tears of sentiment either!

I was always amused by the superfit guns at the bottom of the moor who were warned in advance that the walking was tough going. These guys were always the first ones to collapse breathless into the heather just to "admire the view." It's certainly not for the fainthearted couch potato; in fact, I remember one unfortunate incident when a gun actually collapsed and died in midswing!

You plod onward. The moist autumn air is cool and heavy against your face, but soon you are hot and uncomfortable from the exertion. On the grouse moor, faces quickly turn from sow's belly pink to a shade of turkey-cock red. You reach your allotted grouse butt, and you're grateful for the rest.

A grouse butt is a small, roughly semicircular structure, about three feet high or so, made from rocks and sections of peat turf. Usually a couple of

On the grouse moor, many estates will have something positioned on the top of the butt to prevent the overenthusiastic shooter from allowing his gun to stray in an errant direction toward the neighboring butt to the left or right. THOMAS KIER PHOTO

hazel sticks or something similar are stuck in the top to the left and right to stop the overenthusiastic shooter from swinging through the line.

All that faces you now are vast stretches of purple, sweeping moorland with silver threads of rocky streams tumbling down the almost vertical mountains in the distance. There is an eerie, surreal silence. A bleat of a sheep, or the call of a curlew (or "whaup" as we call them in Scotland), is all that pierces the solitude. For the first time ever, you hear the "bec, bec, go-bec" of an ever-vigilant red grouse that has been watching the proceedings with a beady eye from his tussock of heather. His bright red wattles seem to glow in the watery light of the early morning sun. The morning air is heady with the perfume of heather in full bloom. This is your introduction to the Scottish grouse moor.

An underkeeper brings you your gun and shells. You open the gun, lay it carefully on the heather tussocks on the top of the butt, and empty a box or two of shells into your pouch. The atmosphere is highly charged and your senses tingle with excitement. You peer into the far horizon, and your straining eyes just manage pick out a

pinprick of white on the skyline. You think it's too far, but it's not. The beaters are coming, pushing the birds across the moor from more than two miles away. The specks of white you see are plastic fertilizer sacks tied onto hazel sticks.

As the beaters wave the sticks, the flashing white and the noise the sack makes as it cuts through the air flushes the birds and pushes them toward the waiting guns. A whistle sounds almost inaudibly in the distance, and suddenly you see them, black indistinct specks, smaller than gnats, coming toward you out of the horizon.

You mount the gun at one of the leaders, but you have underestimated his amazing pace; with a whistle of straining pinions, the pack is around your ears and then gone again in an instant before you can turn and take a going away shot. You learn quickly that the ploy is to take the first bird well out in front at a seemingly impossible range and the second as the pack lifts to skim over the butt.

Then (if you have the luxury of shooting a matched pair) change guns and take the next birds behind the line. Be careful here! A swing through the line with the second gun is taboo. The muzzles of the gun should prescribe an overhead arc and then move down with a controlled movement to

A line of beaters will flush the birds toward the waiting guns. THOMAS KIER PHOTO

develop the line of the bird as he hugs the contours of the ground that slopes away from the butt. A hurried, uncontrolled move will result in an erratic poke, and the bird will be gone in the blink of an eye. It's nail-biting, exciting stuff! There may be two or three drives before lunch and another two after. At the end of the day, you have sampled the best, and the experience is locked into your brain forever.

Shooting Driven Birds

There is a specific way to shoot all driven birds. All true driven birds are coming toward your shooting position. On birds like this, developing the line is of the utmost importance because, once again, as soon as the gun comes into your shoulder, the muzzles will try to move horizontally. Driven birds, however, will rarely be moving horizontally relative to your shooting position.

I always tell my clients that a good ploy for developing the line is to imagine a clock face in its usual position flat on a wall. Tall driven pheasants will come over you at 11 o'clock and 1 o'clock. Partridges will often be a bit lower, coming over at 10 o'clock and 2 o'clock. Driven grouse will be lower still at 9 o'clock and 3 o'clock.

Birds that come over you from a true 12 o'clock direction can be shot out in front of you with your weight over your leading leg. However, if you continue to lean forward as the bird approaches (and this is especially true of driven pheasants), it will be impossible to continue your swing past the vertical. As a result, your gun will slow down just as you need extra lead on the bird. To remedy this, you must transfer the weight from your front foot to your back foot. It doesn't take much; just a gentle lift of the heel of the leading leg will suffice, and you will feel the weight transfer to your back leg. Try to do this just as the gun is coming to your face and shoulder. This will give you a more positive swing just when you need vital inches of extra muzzle movement to get in front of the bird.

With a tall incoming pheasant, raise the heel of the leading leg to transfer weight from your front foot to your back foot.

CHAPTER 12

Ducks and Geese

The perils of duck hunting are great . . .

especially for the duck.

—*Walter Cronkite*

Trapped in a crevice of nostalgia, stirring somewhere in the mists of time, are my faded teenage memories of duck and goose hunting forays with my friend Robby. In those days, I would have probably been considered a fanatical wildfowler. When conditions were perfect, I readily abandoned my warm bed in the middle of the night to experience the exhilaration of the fore shore.

Setting off sometimes at 1 o'clock in the morning, I drove my Hillman Minx a hundred miles or so to be on the mudflats and saltings at low tide for the early morning flight, eager for a shot at a mallard, shelduck, or pinkfoot. I was perfectly at home in this hostile environment, with arctic winds scouring the dunes and the whipped-up sand trying hard to find its way through the seams of my clothing. Eyes streaming with tears, nostrils dripping, and fingers numb, I thought nothing of sitting out all night in a muddy gully, deliriously happy in my almost warm clothing and cold, clammy rubber chest waders.

My duck gun was an old 12-gauge AYA No. 3 with 30-inch barrels. I believe the No. 3 was a designation for 3-inch magnum. The shells I used were Czechoslovakian with paper cases in big shot sizes, and they were completely unreliable. One shot would generate an almost gentle shove on the shoulder, and the next would rattle your teeth and leave you wondering what planet you were on. The paper cases responded badly to the slightest drop of moisture. I would sometimes end up feverishly digging the swollen, spent hulls out of the chambers with my pocket knife, just as the sky above me was filled with fat honkers. Often, in the dim light of the gray dawn a long column of flame would spout ominously from the muzzles of the gun with each shot. How those tired old barrels must have stretched at times when I subjected them to those hostile loads!

Robby, my wildfowling companion for many years, was a coalminer in his younger days and later in life a shipyard welder. He wasn't built for the marsh—thin as a pencil with china blue eyes and wavy, steel gray hair. I first saw Robby early one morning, riding his bike down a muddy, pot-holed road that led down to some public wild-fowling marshes on the Humber Estuary. It was a wild night, black as your hat with a cold, driving rain, and I didn't expect to see anyone on the road at that time. I was unprepared for the sudden appearance of a cyclist, wobbling along in the darkness, with a black Labrador trotting alongside. I cursed loudly to myself and swerved to avoid the pair.

Some weeks later, in the damp, gray light of an early Saturday morning, I caught a whiff of ciga-rette smoke long before Robby, slightly the worse for wear from a few drinks from the night before, almost fell into my muddy gully. He was accom-panied by his black Lab, Meg, grayed round the muzzle and arthritic from a hard life on the marsh. I recognized the pair instantly from our previous meeting when I had nearly ran over them in the dark.

During the routine exchange of pleasantries, Robby explained that he lived near the marsh and loved to hunt ducks and geese as much as possible. He wasn't really a pot hunter, but in those days, ducks and the occasional goose were a welcome treat for him and his wife, Annie.

Over the years, I formed a deep attachment to Robby, and we became good wildfowling friends. If the conditions looked good, I would call him late on a Friday night and we would arrange to meet. Robby didn't care if the conditions were good—he would be there anyway. I suspect Robby spent more time on the marsh than anyone else I ever met and what he didn't know about ducks and geese wasn't worth knowing.

He was a skinny guy, but he never complained of the cold. I would tell him there was more meat on a butcher's pencil than there was on him, and he would laugh. I realized later that it was the beer that helped Robby to keep the cold out.

There were no fancy duck calls in those days; Robby could imitate a mallard drake perfectly by sucking on the back of his hand. He didn't call them in; he serenaded them. Robby had three passions in his life: wildfowling, Woodbine ciga-rettes, and Newcastle Brown Ale, probably not in that order. I never even knew his surname—I just never thought to ask, and anyway, it didn't seem necessary.

We would put the decoys out in one of the many creeks and sit down to wait. As soon as the deeks were set, Robby would routinely squint down the barrels of his gun for obstructions, load up a couple of home loads, and prop the old gun up on tussock of marsh grass next to him. Then he would light a cigarette, pull on it deeply, and flick the spent match into the water where it would fizzle and die. I noticed he always did it; over the years it had become a ritual for him.

The ducks were coming; you could feel it. Sometimes, impatient hunters farther along the mudflats would unleash their shots too soon, turn-ing the birds, and Robby would curse under his breath. The chilled arctic air began to bite deeply through the chinks in our clothes, but we waited patiently; we knew our time was coming. Pa-tience, patience, and suddenly, there they were! The sky would come alive with mallards, some of them popping like corks into our decoys where they would stand on their tails and noisily display to summon the others. "Now!" Robby would say, and we would stand in unison to take our birds.

Sometimes we folded two each on that first flight, but that was exceptional.

Robby gave me the foundation to become a successful duck hunter. He always knew where to place the decoys. He always knew where to sit in the wind and where the ducks would come in. Sadly, and quite unexpectedly, one year Robby never returned my calls. I found out later from other fowlers that the days working in the coal mine and the tobacco indulgence eventually took their toll, and Robby succumbed to cancer. I still miss him.

When I first moved to the US in 1997, I managed Westside Sporting Grounds just outside Houston on the Katy Prairie. As the name suggests,

Westside was to the west of Houston on Pederson Road, slap bang in the middle of a unique area. Encompassing a massive sweep of land that borders Houston city limits, the terrain is typical of most of the upper Texas Gulf Coast. Over a thousand square miles, the area is bordered by the Brazos River to the southeast, pine and hardwood forest to the north, and Houston city limits to the east.

Back in the mid-1850s, the Comanche and Karankawa Indians were the first humans to capitalize on the massive buffalo herds that inhabited the prairie, but it was not until the escalation of rice farming in the area in the 1930s that the potential of the wildfowling became apparent. Farming in the 1950s and 1960s increased the rice

The webbed paws, stocky build, and thick, impervious coat of the Labrador retriever make the breed more suitable for retrieving ducks and geese than any other. J. J. KENT PHOTO

production dramatically, and then large quantities of snow geese began arriving. Massive areas of open water, combined with edible waste from the spent rice crops, attracted the geese, which until then had wintered along the marshes on the coast.

Today, in the autumn, when the rice crop has been harvested and the land lies dormant, millions of migratory birds arrive. The variety of species is mind-blowing, and although many of these birds are waders, most of them are waterfowl. The Katy rice fields are their wintering grounds until early March, when they return to their breeding grounds in the Midwest and Canada.

These young aspiring hunters are obviously pleased with themselves! J. J. KENT PHOTOS

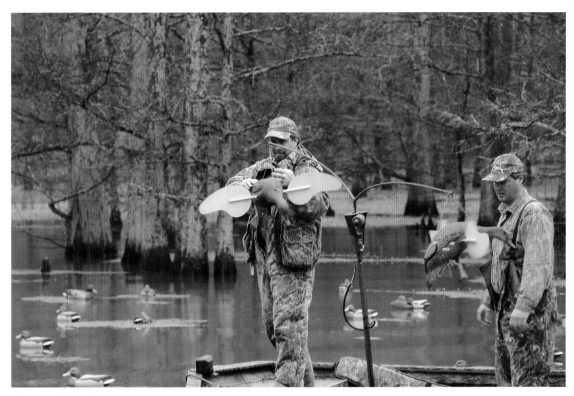

Setting out the decoys. NICK SISLEY PHOTO

During my journey to Westside to work in the mornings, I would marvel at the spectacle of the fallow fields, blanched with thousands of snow geese and interspersed with streaks of speckle bellies and blues. Often I would watch as bald eagles and northern harriers would arrive to quarrel over some of the meager pickings, the occasional wounded birds that had been missed by the hunters. The Katy Prairie has got to be one of the most prolific blue and snow goose locations in the world.

Duck hunting was big in the UK, but I know now that it is revered by many hunters as the main traditional sport in the US. Some states are superior to others, but I think it would be safe to say that there is a prospect of good duck hunting within an hour or two of any major city throughout the US. I now live on Lake Fork in Texas, and as I write, the lake is loaded with wood ducks,

scaup, redheads, and pintails. Because of its diversity, wildfowling (or waterfowling, as you call it here in the US) can also be the most demanding and complicated of the bird hunting sports.

Calls and Decoys

The keen hunter will need a set of duck and goose calls, and he will need to learn how to use them effectively. The only way to do this is to practice, which may drive your wife nuts until you get it right. Ducks aren't stupid; attempting to entice a flock of mallards over your decoy spread with a call that sounds like a wet fart isn't going to work.

You will need sets of decoys too. Years ago they were carved and painted, and today, old duck decoys have become very collectable. I once bought a large sack of hand-carved and painted decoys at a farm sale in Dumfriesshire. They were ancient and weighed a ton. They were riddled with wood-worm, and most of them had faded paint, but some of them were still very lifelike. In the good old days, before the days of television, I suspect some long-gone duck hunter had painstakingly carved them in his leisure evenings for his duck hunting exploits on the Solway Firth. I used them mainly for window decoration in my gun shop, Border Tackle and Guns. I ended up selling them for a modest profit, but I would probably have enough to retire on if I had them today!

Today, with the invention of modern plastics, decoys are lightweight, lifelike, and last indefinitely. A sack full of twenty or so will easily be managed by one person. You will need camouflage nets and, if you decide to go the whole hog, a duck boat and trailer. Then there are the dogs and specialist duck guns.

Evaluating Range

Unless you surprise them, most ducks are shot at extended ranges, and this is where many of us crash and burn. In the past, I have personally killed wind-driven canvasbacks at extended ranges where an estimate of the lead requirement I gave them must have been well in excess of 15 feet! Sometimes with a shot like that, I am surprised, even though I make my living by teaching others to shoot and the figures may prove conclusively that this is, in fact, the amount of lead required. But waterfowling, probably more than any other type of bird hunting, not only has a huge diversity of target species, but also a huge variation of lead requirements, especially at a distance. We see the approach of the speeding greenheads, ghosting over the decoys in the gray light of the morning flight, and give the leader a barrel, only to see the third bird in the pack crumple like yesterday's newspaper. It should tell us something, shouldn't it?

The duck hunter must be able to quickly recognize his quarry. The reason is simple. If you are out pheasant hunting, for example, recognizing a single species is easy. Once you have an idea of how big a pheasant is, you can easily make a pretty good guess at his range. Your brain (depending on your experience in the field) should be able to correlate within reasonable accuracy, the distance of the pheasant at 20 yards, 30 yards, and 40 yards. This is never easy with ducks, because of the diversity of size of the species.

Evaluating range is hard enough, but evaluating range in the sometimes low light conditions of early morning mists is even harder. In the UK, we are allowed to shoot ducks and geese at night, and the best conditions are when there is a small amount of cloud, a thin veil that covers the moon and gives a light background against which the flighting wildfowl is silhouetted. A cloudless sky is too black to silhouette the birds. You may hear them, but most people won't see them until it's too late.

Diversity of Ducks and Geese

After you have served an apprenticeship on the salt marsh or in the duck blind, especially if this time is spent with experienced wildfowler, recognizing species becomes easier. Old hands at the game can recognize each of the species in the blink of an eye. I was lucky to spend many years in a duck blind with Robby, who could spot and recognize ducks long before I could and nudge me to pass on the information. "Here comes a flight of mallards," he would say, or "Lot of pinks coming in; get ready, boy!" and I would still be screwing my eyes up in the early light to spot them.

Identifying ducks by their markings is also important. In the UK, I enjoyed shooting wood pigeons. The woodie has a voracious appetite, and it not only likes quantity, it also likes quality. It is a gregarious bird with the annoying habit of feeding on the best foods: young and tender beans, peas, and fruits. It is a serious agricultural pest. My pigeon shooting mentor in those days was Tom Reed, a tough old Yorkshireman who didn't believe in wasting words . . . or lead shot. What he didn't know about culling woodies wasn't worth knowing.

"Hold your shots, boy—see if he's got a white collar or not," he would say. At first, I never fully understood why. All the birds were pests, so shouldn't we be shooting all of them? Tom's reasoning was twofold: The young birds didn't have the white ring of the clergyman's collar, but the older birds did. Tom had a taste for pigeon pie, and he didn't relish the idea of bringing down a leathery old bird if a younger one was in the cards. The second reason was because by allowing the birds to get near enough to recognize the white collar, we made cleaner kills. The older birds had denser plumage than the younger birds, which reduced the shot penetration and the percentage of pricked birds. After a while, it became easy to quickly recognize the younger birds and make our shots accordingly.

Waterfowl are the same. The white head patch on the bufflehead or the bars on the wings of mallard let the hunter know that the ducks are within range. So just how do we start to learn to recognize them?

Ducks and geese belong to the Anatidae family. All ducks have rapid, constant wing beats to propel their rather heavy-looking bodies. Larger ducks have slower wing beats than the smaller ones. They have short tails, long necks, and long bills.

The Anatinae is a subfamily of Anatidae containing dabbling ducks that feed in water and on land on small lakes, ponds, and grain fields instead of diving. They are fond of grain crops, insects, and some root vegetables. Fallow carrot and potato fields are good areas. Mallards (probably harvested by hunters more than any other duck), pintail, shoveller, wood duck, and both blue- and green-wing teal are examples of dabblers.

Diving ducks in the subfamily Aythyinae feed by diving under the water. Examples are scaups, redheads, and canvasback ducks. These ducks rise out of the water and flap their wings, tipping their tails up in the shallows, and preen noisily and vigorously. All diving ducks have an even more rapid wing beat than dabblers, and to become airborne, they run across the surface. Dabblers can take off vertically from the surface and become airborne within a flap or two of their wings.

There are two main duck hunting methods: from a blind, with a good dose of well positioned decoys and the help a duck call, and pass shooting, where the birds fly to and from their feeding grounds.

Making a quick identification is common sense, but it trips up many hunters, who get confused by the speed and size of the birds. If, for example, you know the bird coming in is a mallard, you will be able to decide when he's in range and know exactly when you need to take your shot. But if the bird is a blue-wing teal and you don't recognize that, he will be on you and then gone in an instant before you will get the gun to your shoulder. By the same rule, after killing one of the larger ducks, such as a mallard at 40 yards, you might let a diminutive teal go past at 30 yards because you believe it is out of range.

When I was younger and I hunted in Scotland, conversations with some of the older guys revealed that they saw lead in bird lengths. For example, a mallard that is crossing in front of us at a distance of 40 yards or so is a six-duck length. Once again, recognition played a big part here. Some duck hunters swear they see lead in duck lengths, but I was never able do that with any conviction.

Reading the speed of larger ducks is tricky. Reading the speed of geese is even trickier. Years ago my wife and I managed a shooting facility in Devon, in the south of England. The facility was a stone's throw from the coast, and the area was frequented by lots of Canada geese. The Devon and Cornwall area was a popular destination for hordes of holiday makers from London and other inner-city dwellers.

Many of the holiday facilities had invested in stock ponds that were filled with rainbow trout as an added attraction for the holiday makers. All these trout were farm-raised, pellet-fed fish that couldn't tell the difference between a protein pellet and a Canada goose dropping, which is highly toxic. Sometimes if the weather turned nasty on the coast, the Canadas would fly inland at dusk with the intention of roosting and feeding overnight on the more sheltered inland waters of the trout lakes. At first, the effect of these nocturnal visitors went unnoticed, but eventually after the combined overnight ablutions of several hundred Canada geese, the trout would become sick and die. Steps were taken by the local authorities to expose the culprits, and the fingers of blame were pointed at the geese.

As luck would have it, the holiday complex my wife and I managed was right on the flight path between the Tamar Lakes and Clovelly Country Club. As a bit of sport for the guests, we would pass shoot the geese as they came in at dusk, and again in the morning as they returned to the coastal mudflats. It was all great fun, but it quickly became obvious to me that most of the guest guns were struggling to connect with the geese because they miscalculated their range. Canadas are big geese. At 50 yards they are still within range and vulnerable to your gun. At 80 yards they still look big, but they are not within range. Anything short of a lucky shot with an elephant gun won't bring him down. So to prevent more geese from being pricked and wounded, I devised a plan. I made a life-size plywood cutout of a Canada goose and gave it a realistic coat of paint. Each week, as the new guests arrived, I would test their range-finding capabilities. The Canada goose replica worked amazingly well. Within a short space of time, clients could estimate the yardage to the plywood goose reasonably accurately, in some cases to within a few yards. More birds were bagged and killed cleanly as a result.

Big birds need big guns and loads. NICK SISLEY PHOTO

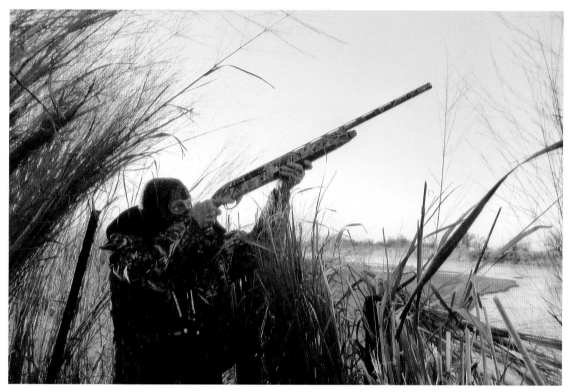

Ducks and geese have amazing eyesight. Good camouflage and a good blind is essential. WALT KILGO PHOTO

At the start of this chapter I explained that I managed a facility on the Katy Prairie. One morning, as I was travelling along the approach road to the facility, I clocked a flock of speckle bellies battling a strong headwind, but despite this, the geese were still travelling at over 50 miles per hour. From the ground, for a distance of about a hundred yards or so, it appeared that they were hardly moving.

Ducks have excellent vision. When I was a kid, I used to fish a lot and dig worms for bait in the midden (dung heap) at my uncle's farm. Within minutes, I would be surrounded by several white, intelligent-looking domesticated ducks. With pinpoint, beady-eyed accuracy, those ducks would spot a miniscule movement, hidden in the diggings, and grab the worms long before I could. It's the same with wildfowl. As they fly over your decoys, they have the uncanny ability to locate that

flash of your face as you risk squinting into the wide blue yonder when you're convinced they're not looking. Then you wonder why they flare like Harrier jets and land in the next county.

I was sitting in a blind one day at Eagle Lake, and I jokingly mentioned to my hunting buddy that the ducks were keeping out of range because they could see what shot size he was using. "How do they know that?" he asked. I replied that they could read it on the sides of the red spent hulls that were littered around the edges of the duck blind.

Don't forget that anything you can see on the ground that may look suspect will be compounded by the ducks' and geese's aerial view. Remove anything that is out of place, including decoy sacks, shell boxes, gun slips, thermos flasks, and sandwich boxes. The ducks will see these things and flare away from the area.

Knowing Your Place

With duck hunting, you need to be in the right place at the right time. Good planning can make all the difference between a fruitful trip and one where the dog snores the day away as you sit in the blind until your butt is cold and numb.

Most species of ducks, both puddlers and divers, respond well to decoys and calling, but the common mallard and perhaps the scaup, in my opinion, respond the best. It is wise to know your terrain, and when hunting large lake areas, it pays to take the time to analyze your situation, especially wind direction, before you put the decoys out. Lots of overeager hunters abandon objectivity and pick the wrong spot.

Take some binoculars and try to spot where the birds are feeding. If you see an area that has airborne birds over it and also pockets of birds on the water, the ducks obviously know something that you don't and are attracted to that area. Logically, it may be worth setting up in that area. Sometimes, with careful observation, it is possible to spot these pockets of birds in the early light at exceptional distances. I consider my eyesight good, not exceptional, but I can spot duck and goose activity at well over 2 to 3 miles in clear conditions. The trick is to locate the birds and drive toward them at the same time.

Too many hunters worry about scaring ducks just as it gets light. If it is early enough, don't worry too much at this stage; ducks that are disturbed often return to feed after the decoys have been set. If you have several setup locations to pick from and several blinds to select from, don't automatically favor one without checking the water for birds

This is what ducks should see as they come into the decoys. Nothing looks suspicious or out of place.

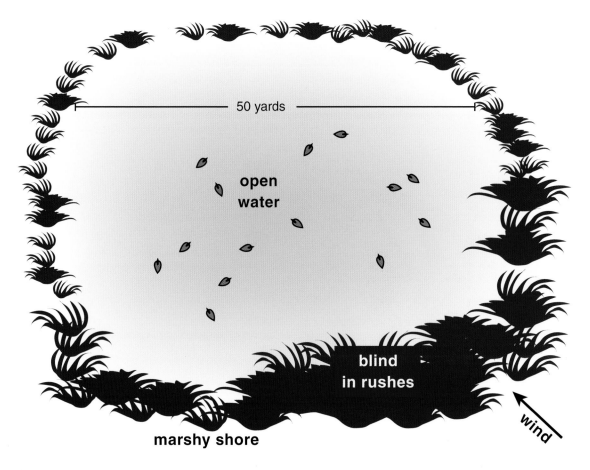

A sheltered area like this one—a small cove off the main body of water—may be a more productive spot to set the decoys out.

first. Don't be tempted to throw all the decoys out into an "easy" area because it is close and accessible and you don't feel like walking far. A close and unimaginative concentration of decoys will not encourage the ducks to land among them. If possible, wade into different areas to position several small groups of thinly spaced decoys instead of one large patch that is tightly packed.

Wind Direction

Wind direction plays a big part. Decoys placed in choppy areas may be unproductive; ducks prefer the leeward side of cover and will fly into the de-

coys more or less facing the wind. Ducks don't like to feed and display in areas with heavy water disturbance.

I personally prefer the ducks to come in toward me because I always think that this type of setup will present easier shots as the ducks flare to land, especially if they are dabblers and not divers. After they detect the first shot or movement from the blind, dabblers will instantly lift off again, rising almost vertically, and these shots are the easiest in my opinion.

Some duck hunters I have hunted with favor instead ducks that come in across the wind so that the shots are taken from the side. Divers, however, will track across the surface and take off into a cross wind. Once again, I think these are the easiest shots to take. If you favor a cross wind setup, take into account whether you are a left- or right-handed shooter. In the past I have carefully distributed decoys only to find that as the ducks come in my swing is restricted by part of the blind.

Don't restrict your swing. Careful planning of a duck blind location can help even the odds.

The end of a perfect day.

Guns

Gun selection for the duck and goose hunter is simple. Although I favor a double gun for most of my upland hunting, I feel that waterfowling is one area where the semiautomatic shines. The gun can be loaded far more easily than a break-action double in the confines of a duck blind. Most ducks and geese call for heavier shells, and recoil from an over-and-under or side-by-side can be prohibitive for those sensitive to it. As the breech blot of the semi is driven rearward with the detonation of the shell, the recoil is spread over a longer period, resulting in steady push on the shooter's shoulder instead of a sharp blow. Anybody who has tried to shoot multiple shots with a 7 1/2-pound upland bird 12 gauge will know exactly what I'm talking about here!

A word of warning: I regularly see duck hunters loading semiautomatics by pushing the shells into the chambers with their thumbs. This isn't necessary. Regardless of where the shell is dropped into the breech, when the bolt release button is pushed, the action will pick the shell up and efficiently load it. I have seen a shooter load a shell and accidentally hit the bolt release on the side of the receiver with his knuckle, slamming the bolt forward onto his thumb. Very painful!

I still shoot ducks and geese, but not as much now as I once did. It's not that I don't enjoy it, but as I'm getting on in years, I want to be more comfortable and leave it for the younger guys. Some hunters will tell you that dove hunting is the most difficult form of shotgunning. Others insist that it's driven pheasant or quail. I feel that quality duck hunting, because of the extreme wariness of the birds, the often hostile conditions, and the extreme ranges, comes close to the pinnacle of shotgunning perfection. The successful duck hunter, in my opinion, represents the true expert.

CHAPTER 13

Woodcock and Ruffed Grouse

Here on the Island,
They're mostly passing through,
One night stand woodcock,
So casual hardly anyone aware.

—*Marnie Crowell*

The woodcock is a bird of oak woodlands, boggy field bottoms, and brushy field margins. The bird is well-suited to this environment; its plumage is a speckled pattern of russets and browns, which blends perfectly with the spent and rotting leaves of a forest floor. With its rounded wings, large head, and protruding eyes, it always reminds me of a large, brown moth. Both the woodcock and the ruffed grouse are favorites of mine from a sporting shot point of view, not a culinary one, but more about that later.

You can easily find woodcock feeding areas. Farmland, especially farmland with either apple orchards or peach orchards, can be particularly productive, because these places usually have a good crop of worms. Stands of saplings with sycamore, alder, and willow are also favored, as are bracken-clad hillsides and briar thickets.

I live on Lake Fork in east Texas, and in mid–November 2010, the lake was about 4 feet below its normal level. Some mornings when I walked the shoreline with my dogs, the mud around the low water areas was covered with small holes. Many of these holes were the work of Wilson's snipe, a smaller cousin of the woodcock, but there were others where the woodcock also had been driving their beaks into the ground in search of worms.

I saw the telltale white droppings that woodcock hunters call chalk. In mid–November I often see woodcock sign in this area in young pine plantations. The woodcock drop into these places under cover of darkness, migrating down from the Midwestern states by the light of the moon. These areas are difficult to hunt, with nearly impenetrable thickets of cat's claw briar, blackberry, and infant conifers. Even though woodcock prefer damp ground, I have never had much success around the perimeter of stagnant water, and I have no explanation for this.

The Wily Woodcock

Woodcock move around a lot, and I consider the wily woodcock to be the most secretive of birds, appearing like ghostly apparitions in droves overnight and vanishing just as quickly without a trace the next. Sometimes it's obvious that several dozen birds have been feeding in the area, sometimes there are none. I have flushed woodcock on several occasions when out with my dogs in the mornings. Often I have tried to sneak down to the lake in the evening without the dogs to observe them as they fly in. Very few hunters shoot them here; at this time of the year most Texans are preoccupied with quail.

I remember my first woodcock as if it were yesterday. Years ago, I was a member of a syndicate shoot in the north of England. In those days, small syndicates paid a modest price to a benevolent farmer in the area and managed all the shooting on it themselves. In return they would control the rabbit population or any other vermin on the land. The farmer was invited to shoot on a guest day. The downside to the syndicate was that the members had to do all the work required for the successful release of the game. Most had a full-time occupation, so evenings and weekends were the only times this was possible.

Some of the older members knew the favored woodcock haunts, and one area that always seemed productive was a tangle of blackberry briars, elderberry, and alders that ran along the sides of a deep gully with a stream at the bottom.

The area along the stream was seriously overgrown, completely impenetrable, but they would send the dogs down to flush the birds, knowing from experience that this usually worked. As another syndicate member and I walked the sides of the gully with our dogs working below us, I heard the shout from him, "Woodcock forward!" He unselfishly gave me the best chance of a shot.

I was a fairly new syndicate member and until that day, never shot a woodcock. It was a highly charged situation, and in the heat of the moment my gun came up and I dropped the bird as dead as a stone. I was a good shot, but as I walked forward to retrieve the bird, my elation quickly evaporated as I stooped to pick up the crumpled body of a young little owl. As I picked the beautiful bird up, limp and lifeless, I was desperately sorry for what I had done. The warm body was beaded with ruby spots of blood. The coloration of the plumage, size of the owl, and the ghosting flight pattern was similar to a woodcock's, and I convinced myself that it was an easy mistake to make. But little owls were rare in this area; I had committed a cardinal sin and destroyed one.

I can vividly remember that moment as though it were yesterday. Every instant, even to the extent that I know the bird saw me at exactly the same time that I squeezed the trigger, is indelibly etched onto my hard drive. Over the next several days, the painful memory started to fade, but even now over thirty years later, I still remember it. The experience taught me one thing that I have never forgotten. I was desperate to bag a woodcock, and being so eager, I shot at something that I didn't recognize. With the owl it was an easy, but very regrettable mistake to make, but it proved to me that in the heat of the moment a normally careful shotgunner can be seduced into taking a shot that he shouldn't make.

Later that same morning I did bag my first woodcock. The bird appeared unexpectedly at the end of an alder thicket, and I shot him cleanly and safely as he popped over the low trees. It was

a day to remember, filled equally with both re-
morse and elation.

Woodcock have a tendency to bring out the
worst in a shooting man from a safety point of
view. When out woodcocking, never be tempted
to take a low shot as a bird swoops down to land
behind a tangle of briars or a leafy thicket. It's not
worth the risk.

If you do let off a safe shot as a bird does this,
this downward swoop to drop back into cover can
be misleading. More than once, I have been fooled
into thinking that the bird was hit, and after sending the dog to pick the bird, I have watched him
flit away into the shadows completely unscathed.

When a bird drops back into cover suddenly
and you haven't fired a shot, mark the spot, check
your dog, and try to avoid walking in on him immediately. Leave him for a minute or two so that
he can settle down first because, as he settles and as
your dog moves in again to point him, you will
gain a split-second advantage as he loses the element of surprise. The second and more important
reason is that you'll gain time to mark the location
of your companions so that as he flushes, the shot
will be in a safe direction.

In my opinion, the woodcock has a more unpredictable flight pattern than any bird. Like a
pheasant's breast feather caught in a uplifting wind
current, he has a flight pattern that I can best describe only as a corkscrewing, zigzag flight pattern.
He doesn't do this very fast, but he will zig while
your muzzle zags, which can frustrate even a good
shot. There is no predicting which direction a
woodcock will take, unlike quail. Most times, it's a
safe bet that he will be moving in a direction that
is generally away from you, and as he touches the
treetops, he will hang in the air for an instant as if
to decide where he's going next. That is exactly
the time to take your shot.

Most woodcock hunters react too quickly to
the appearance of the bird, making a poke-and-
pray shot. The birds are not fast flyers; their secret
and defense is their aerial agility, but it isn't fast
like a dove.

The cover you hunt woodcock in will be the
densest and toughest imaginable. Scotland was bad
enough, and you work hard for the birds there, but
in Texas you work a darn sight harder! Warm,
tough clothing is essential, but depending on your
location, you should avoid dressing too warmly.
The areas where you will find the woodcock will

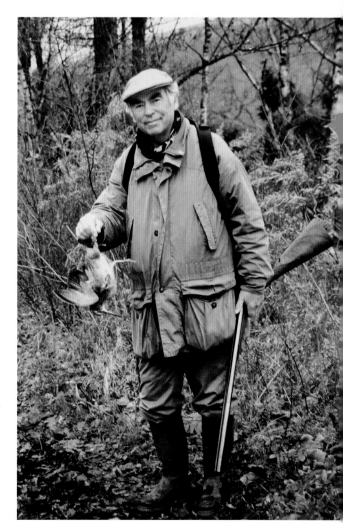

A nice woodcock taken from a classic location. DR. PAUL
ZENDHER PHOTO

be dense cover with little wind penetration; pushing slowly through this type of cover takes more energy than you think, and you will become hot and tired quickly.

The best time for action is early morning when the birds, mainly nocturnal feeders, are still active.

In thick cover and low light conditions, the broad sighting plane of the side-by-side (above) can stand out better than the over-and-under (below).

If a flight of birds has arrived overnight, they will often feed close together. If one bird is flushed unexpectedly, it's a safe bet that there is another one or two nearby. Most times, the bird will rise to the top of the cover that you flush him out of, and this is usually the best chance of a shot because the shot is a perfectly safe one and the bird will hesitate and hang in the air just for an instant, as if deciding which direction to take.

I have flushed woodcock on occasion from really thick cover, so close that they almost flew into me. The problem then isn't really the speed you can get the gun up but the fact that it may be difficult to do this; cat's claw, brambles, saplings, and the like will all hamper your swing.

Most woodcock will flush close, so a 20 gauge with 8 shot will do. I don't like semiautos for woodcock, although some shooters favor them so that they can get as much lead in the air as possible. In my opinion, a short-barreled double is better because you won't have many chances when you will be able to safely let off more than two shots. I like a side-by-side for this type of hunting in low light conditions in thick cover. Something like an open-choked quail gun would be perfect.

Finally, due to the mostly impenetrable cover you will be hunting through, don't ever be tempted to take a fancy gun woodcock hunting. The one I use now is a beat-up old 26-inch barreled Browning Citori skeet gun. In the UK I often used a side-by-side AYA that is just as beat up. I found that on some of the dark overcast days I had a distinct advantage with the more distinct sighting plane of the side-by-side over the narrower visual peripheral picture of the over-and-under. In the US, many ruffed grouse hunters prefer the side-by-side for exactly that reason.

I always regret admitting this, but I think woodcock are the most unpalatable birds for the table. The first woodcock that I ever shot in Scotland was "expertly" prepared and cooked for me at a syndicate dinner. The traditional way to present a woodcock for the table is to pluck the bird and then pan-roast it in port wine. Note that I said the complete bird. That includes everything, even the entrails. The woodcock is then served on a slice of garlic toast with the juices from the cooking process poured over the top. The correct presentation of this gourmet dish for the table, I was assured, called for the bird to still have both legs intact and—I kid you not!—the beak of the bird inserted up its backside. I do eat the woodcock I shoot, but not whole. I breast them and mix the cubed breast meat with other game birds to make game pie.

Ruffed Grouse

A companion bird to the woodcock is the ruffed grouse, the most widespread and most sought-after species of grouse in America. The ruffed grouse is a good table bird, with white, succulent meat, similar to chicken, and there is no doubt that this was his downfall. Apparently in some of the northern portions of good grouse habitat, it was considered a staple of residents' diet, and a daily bag of 30 birds was not unusual. There is no doubt that this ruthless persecution by pot hunters contributed to the ghosting instincts of the grouse today.

I believe that the ruffed grouse is the most elusive game bird there is. My experience has been that I and like-minded others will take an insane, irrational delight in pursuing them through impossible terrain. We continue until we are exhausted, and the dog is even more exhausted. We look as though we have done battle with a man-eating tiger as we push our way doggedly through the chokeberries, brambles, and thorns. Then, if our luck is good, we may see four birds all day. The ones we actually have a go at have the uncanny knack of exploding from under cover on our favorite trail just as we straddle an overgrown log and try hard to castrate ourselves. It never fails, does it?

His Scottish cousin, the wary, elusive red grouse, relies on camouflage and fast flying to evade his pursuer, but the ruffed grouse is the master of illusion, an absolute expert at putting a tree between itself and your gun.

We don't have ruffed grouse in Scotland, and I was told when I first hunted them here that a few decades ago market hunting was common. I believe that just like the red grouse in the Scottish Highlands (who when walking up can always spot you long before you spot them), the ruffed grouse has acquired the ability to resort to evasive action from generations of hunting by market gunners. You can see this taking place if you hunt the same areas on a regular basis. The early season birds will hold well to a point, and you will harvest some. But some of these birds seem to have a rapid learning curve, and every time you cover the same ground as the season progresses, the birds will be a mite more skittish and hug the ground so low as they fly that a shot is impossible. I firmly believe that human predation can breed a dose of shotgun savvy into each generation. Of course, new birds come into the area, but there always seems to be one or two older birds that are the masters of illusion, flushing in complete silence and expertly dodging behind the sanctuary of the aspens just as you are about to take a shot.

You can use the same gun and load on grouse that you do on woodcock. Because the grouse is a larger bird than the woodcock (about two pounds to the woodcock's half pound), go up a size with the shot, instead of 8s for the woodcock, to $7\frac{1}{2}$ for the grouse. A fast-handling skeet gun or 20-gauge side-by-side is ideal, with wide open chokes. Grouse won't be shot at ranges greater than 25 to 30 yards, I promise you!

Index